# Encountering Jesus

# Encountering Jesus

Zan W. Holmes, Jr.

Foreword by William B. McClain

*Abingdon Press*
Nashville

ENCOUNTERING JESUS

*Copyright © 1992 by Abingdon Press*

Leader's Guide prepared by John D. Schroeder.

*This book is printed on acid-free, recycled paper.*

**Library of Congress Cataloging-in-Publication Data**

Holmes, Zan W., 1935–
    Encountering Jesus/Zan W. Holmes; foreword by William B.
    McClain.
        p.   cm.
    Includes bibliographical references.
    **ISBN 0-687-08572-1** (alk. paper)
        1. Jesus Christ—Person and offices. 2.  Christian life—1960–
    3.  Church renewal. 4.  Holmes, Zan W., 1935–      . I.  Title.
    II. Series.
    BT202.H595      1992
    232'.8—dc20                                                            92-3673
                                                                               CIP

03 04 05 — 15 14 13 12

MANUFACTURED IN THE UNITED STATES OF AMERICA

This book is dedicated to the Grace of God
as I have experienced it in my father,
the Reverend Zan Wesley Holmes, Sr.;
my mother, Naomi Ruth Holmes;
my wife, Dorothy Burse Holmes;
and the members of the faithful and vital
congregation at
St. Luke "Community" United Methodist Church,
Dallas, Texas.

# CONTENTS

## A C K N O W L E D G M E N T S

This book could not have been written without my friend and colleague Dr. William B. McClain, Professor of Preaching and Worship at Wesley Theological Seminary, Washington, D.C. He read the manuscript and provided many valuable insights and suggestions that were incorporated into the final version.

I am also grateful to Dr. Theodore Walker, Assistant Professor of Ethics and Society at Perkins School of Theology in Dallas. A gifted theologian and member of St. Luke "Community" United Methodist Church, he provided helpful and challenging feedback.

I thank Jo Ann Mattos McClain and Ann I. Ralston for the use of their competent word processing skills.

Finally, for helping me to cover the local church base while I spent time on this book, I am indebted to my core staff at St. Luke "Community" United Methodist Church.

Z an Holmes, one of the church's most effective preachers and pastors, has written much in this book, which the whole church needs to read: clergy, youth, teachers, and lay adults. Drawing on his own considerably broad and rich experience, he has helped us to see the need to drink fresh water from old springs.

In *Encountering Jesus* he offers practical and helpful suggestions and reflections on how our churches can, in fact, become faithful and vital in a time when so many of our pastors and their congregations feel helpless and hopeless. And he does it with a simple profundity and a deep sense of caring for the problems of our times and the resources and grace the church can offer "in Christ's name."

While this book contains many insights from biblical material and theological disciplines, it is written primarily by a practical pastor who has faced the need of a local church to show signs of vitality. And, although he writes out of his experience in the African American church, what he shares with his readers is discernment and insight for any church that would seek to be faithful to the call to be a society of the friends of Jesus.

Much like his forebears and following in a long line of preachers, Dr. Holmes's passion for preaching and worship comes through. He is one whose "zeal has not flagged." And there are points in the book where the preacher's voice is heard with clarion urgency trying to bring the gospel to bear on human need—sounding a note of prophetic exigency now, whispering a word of grace after a thunderous denunciation of our sinful predicament, issuing a tender love call to return home, and continually hauntingly inviting us to have "an encounter with Jesus." One can feel the preacher's sense of joy about his own encounter with Jesus, and it shows in the enervating and energizing nature of the author's own piety without piousness. He does not hide the fact that he wants to tell the story of a God who searches and haunts and wants back what belongs to that God—even those in the far country. His passionate call for preaching is matched only by his ardent plea for congregations to participate in the preaching: "preaching congregations and listening pastors"—a novel way of describing a sound and sensible idea, historically and theologically.

But the preacher is no mere evangel of a comfortable place in the solemn assembly, spiritual inebriation, or mere "feel good religion." Nor does he spend a great deal of time on stressing personal morality, as if that would solve our problems. Throughout the book there is a consistent reminder of the holy nature of the God we encounter, the corporate nature of sin, and the utter necessity of balancing celebration and praise with lives of sacrifice and service, which are achieved not merely with acts of charity but with the demands to actively seek justice.

The author of this book is authentic. I say so for three reasons: (1) He is willing to make confession of his own errors and struggles to be a good minister of the church of Jesus Christ, and reports his failures as well as his triumphs. (2) He does not try to write a "how-to" book (of which we have far too many) or an esoteric gnostic theological treatise (which most would not read), but he speaks out of a sense of "This is what happened to me in my ministry and with my congregation." And there are many anecdotes and "real people" to help us feel with him the real life situations. And, (3) I know that what he writes about at St. Luke "Community" Church is a living, vital experience that continues. I have recently had the privilege and honor of participating with that congregation and minister as visiting preacher/author/ teacher, but more important, as a parent of one of his young adult members who "went back to church" because there was a vital congregation. As he put it: "Dad, this is a church where things are happening and everybody wants to be involved in the church *and* the community!" That, for me, is testimony enough.

At a time when the apparently prevailing voices say a God who sides with the poor and the oppressed is either hidden or absent or is no longer interested, this pastor/teacher offers assurance that we can still catch a vision of the Caring One in the crowded ways of life. He is confident that we can hear that Voice above the noises of race, violence, marketplace theology, strife, and even the solemn assembly.

I am glad Zan Holmes has agreed to share that story and his insights and wisdom with a larger audience. And he does so without an ego-obsession or telling a "bragging tale." There is much in what he has written in *Encountering Jesus* to help an ailing church find healing, to help a hopeless people find the promise of vision and grace, to help struggling pastors with struggling congregations take heart and courage, and for all of us to have a fresh *encounter with Jesus that counts!*

William B. McClain
*Professor of Preaching and Worship*
*Wesley Theological Seminary*
*Washington, D.C.*

# Encounters That Count

T he late Howard Thurman, for many years the Dean of Rankin Chapel at Howard University and later Marsh Chapel at Boston University, used to tell about an experience he had when he visited Mahatma Gandhi in India. While there he was asked to preach at a Christian mission in New Delhi. Thurman had been chosen by *Time* magazine as one of the top ten preachers in America, and by the accounts of all who heard him, he was a great preacher. The Indian mission was anxious to hear him, and he accepted the invitation. After he finished preaching a sermon that he felt he had delivered with effectiveness and authority and was removing his vestments, he thought he would seek confirmation from the young Indian Christian who had heard him and was helping him replace his jacket. The young man assured him that he had done a fine job, but the Indian Christian started to cry. Surprised and confused by this unexpected reaction, Thurman asked,

"But why are you crying? I thought you said that you enjoyed the sermon and you appreciated my message. You said that it was profound and well-delivered and even eloquent." The young man replied, "Yes, Dr. Thurman, all of that is true. But you did not call his name. I wanted to hear you call the name of Jesus!"

Some years ago, the church I am now pastoring was going through what we all decided was "a spiritual crisis." I asked our council on ministries to come together to make an assessment and to begin to set some goals for our church. It seemed that we were experiencing a decline in attendance and a concomitant lack of enthusiasm about worship and our work as the church. Although we were doing many social programs with a good degree of success, our choirs and organizations were functioning, the fellowship seemed to be warm and caring, and I was preaching what most people who attended agreed were well-constructed and well-delivered sermons, something seemed to be missing.

After two days of intensive conversation, ardent engagement, soul-searching dialogue, reflective analysis, and fervent prayer, we concluded that our problem was spiritual—the Bible did not figure heavily into our life and work and worship, except as a reference point on occasion. We had forgotten to allow ourselves to remember that what we were doing was to be done in his name! We had allowed ourselves to slip into a "Jesus Institution" without encountering Jesus—an encounter that really counts. We had become more concerned about appearances and success and numbers and order than being a church that saw every gathering—whether worship, committee or board meeting, community action for change, or counseling session—as an opportunity to experience Jesus, sometimes as healer/comforter/friend, sometimes as justifier, sometimes as sanctifier, sometimes as liberator/seeker of justice, but always as the Christ of God whose "name is above every name."

The council on ministries decided to write a mission statement together that captured the essentials of the faith. After much soul-searching, Bible study, and discussion concerning the meaning of the faith and prayer, we developed the following words of communal affirmation, which the council on ministries perfected and the whole congregation adopted:

> In the name of Jesus Christ, who is made known to us through the Holy Scriptures, and by the inspiration of the Holy Spirit, we are called to establish, maintain, and nurture a personal relationship with God. We are also called to be a community of God's caring people, within the church and world community, by serving as faithful stewards of our time, talents, and money; by combating injustice wherever it may exist; by implementing outreach ministries to meet the needs of the total community; and by our evangelistic witness to the Saviorhood of Jesus Christ in all that we say and do.

These words became an affirmation of faith, which the congregation often repeats at its services of worship. It is included in every printed bulletin or program. Every activity or ministry is measured by the criteria of this missional statement and periodically reviewed and assessed. It is a reminder each time we come together that we gather "in Christ's name!" It is a way of remembering who we are and rehearsing acts of grace that have transformed us and renewed us. It helps us recall the Spirit of God who calls us to live creatively and constructively and find meaning and purpose in our daily lives; the Spirit sends us forth into the world to witness and to serve.

It was interesting for me to note that it was at a retreat that we were confronted with the need to be more intentional in our encounters. For part of what the congregation was saying was: "Sir, we would see Jesus." While they were not decrying social programs and well-organized sermons and efficient organization and fine fellowship, those are not enough unless we are continually made aware of why we are doing what we are doing. When that awareness is absent, then we may as well go to some club or fraternity or service institution to do some things and enjoy warm fellowship. They were saying what the young Indian Christian was saying to Dr. Thurman: "Call his name!" For it is in his name that we become transformed and witness to the power of his grace in the daily triumphs of our lives; it is in Christ's name that we become alive in worship, faith, and service as vital Christians. We become his followers, own up to his cause, and dare to speak his name.

To encounter Jesus is to take on the name of Christ. During a sermon preached at our congregation, Dr. William B. McClain, Professor of Preaching and Worship at Wesley Theological Seminary in Washington, D.C., told the story of meeting a South Korean tailor in Itaewon, Seoul, named Smitty Lee. When Dr. McClain asked whether the name "Smitty" was Korean, the tailor told the story of his life being saved during the

Korean War by an American soldier from Virginia who was called Smitty Ransom. The tailor further explained a rather familiar custom in that Asian culture, and summed it up in two simple sentences: "He saved my life. I took his name." That is indeed what happens when we encounter Jesus; he saves our lives, and we take his name.

But where and how do we encounter Jesus in these modern days? Shall we expect to be knocked off a horse and become blinded and led to Strait Street to regain our sight and leave with a new vision for our lives? Shall we wait for an entourage of ten thousand legions of angels to escort him into our weary and confused presence? Shall we look for a new star and linger on the bosom of the night until Jupiter comes in contact with Saturn creating a natural nocturnal constellation of light that may lead us to a new appearance of Christ? No, I believe that he can step across the centuries and into our time and stand among us in his risen power. We can encounter him in familiar places: in the Bible, no matter which translation is used; in worship as we gather, whether only two or three, or four or five thousand; in the sacraments—in baptism, whether by immersion, pouring, or sprinkling; in the Eucharist, whether by intinction or drinking from the cup—in the life of the church and its work, no matter where the people gather; and in the world that God loved and loves so much. What Albert Schweitzer wrote many years ago is still a powerful word and witness:

> He comes to us as One unknown, without a name, as of old, by the lakeside. He came to those men who knew Him not. He speaks to us the same word: "Follow thou

me!" and sets us to the tasks which He has to fulfill for
our time. He commands. And to those who obey Him,
whether they be wise or simple, He will reveal Himself
in the toils, the conflicts, the sufferings which they shall
pass through in His fellowship, and, as an ineffable
mystery, they shall learn in their own experience Who
He is.[1]

Some may use other names. But it is Jesus of
Nazareth, the Founder of the church, whom we
encounter, and when we have an encounter with him it
is an encounter that counts! To some he is the grand
representation of all the distilled longings of humankind
for fulfillment, for perfection, for wholeness, for
satisfaction. To some he is Eternal Presence hovering
over all the many needs of our broken humanity,
yielding healing and health for the sick of body and soul,
and giving a lift to those who have grown weary in the
long pilgrimage. But, as Howard Thurman said almost
fifty years ago in *Jesus and the Disinherited*, "to some he
is more than a Presence; he is the God fact, the Divine
Moment in human sin and misery. . . . He becomes the
Man most worthy of honor and praise" (p. 112). Dr.
Thurman goes on to say in the most simple and eloquent
words: "He belongs to no age, no race, no creed. When
we look into his face, we see etched the glory of our own
possibilities, and our hearts whisper, 'Thank you and
thank God!' "

Being faithful is about encountering this Jesus in the
ordinary places—the familiar places of the Bible, the
sanctuary, the celebration of the sacraments, the
preached Word of God within and outside of the

Temple, the committee meetings, and the marketplace of the world where liberating justice is sought as the very will of God that the next few pages are devoted. Christian life is about encountering Jesus, the exchange we have with God.

This book is about the kind of undressing/redressing encounter David had with God. God's grace makes it King David's finest hour! It was arrogance, not his sex drive, that drove David to claim Uriah's wife. After all, David already had several wives, so what is one more to be added to his harem; adultery was not the issue—but arrogance, pride, and murder were. He was clearly wearing the garments of arrogance and self-righteousness, which are symbolized in his seeing himself above the law of God; in David's heart God had been dethroned and replaced by self. But when David heard the Word that God sent to undress him from his clothes of arrogance and self-righteousness, he did not respond by covering up with lying to conceal more clothes of arrogance and self-righteousness. Instead, David slipped off his throne, fell on his knees, and said:

> Have mercy on me, O God,
>   according to your steadfast love;
> according to your abundant mercy
>   blot out my transgressions.
> Wash me thoroughly from my iniquity,
>   and cleanse me from my sin.
> For I know my transgressions,
>   and my sin is ever before me.
> Create in me a clean heart, O God,
>   and put a new and right spirit within me.
> Restore to me the joy of your salvation. . . .

> Then I will teach transgressors your ways,
> and sinners will return to you.
> (Psalm 51:1-3, 10, 12-13)

This was an encounter that counted. My forebears put it something like this: anywhere we give him our garments of sorrow, God gives us the robe of joy. In exchange for the armor of confusion, God gives us the armor of peace. In exchange for our twisted image of self-righteousness, God gives us an open, trusting, and redeemed self. To encounter Jesus and to have an exchange with God is the real business of the church, and it counts!

I still find myself marveling at the testimony of Richard Allen, one of the earliest Methodists and later the founder of the African Methodist Episcopal Church. Allen said when he was first introduced to Jesus by a Methodist preacher, "I cried unto him who delightest to hear the prayers of a poor sinner, and all of a sudden my dungeon shook, my chains flew off, and glory to God, I cried. My soul was filled. I cried, enough for me—the Savior died."

This book is written to explore how we encounter Jesus in new ways, in old familiar places, as persons and as congregations. It is my hope that it will help individuals and our churches experience a new vitality in their lives. I am certain that it is possible. Let it be so.

# Encountering Jesus
# in the Bible

From the beginning of the church, Christians have been "a people of the book." In *Shaped by the Bible*, William H. Willimon labors to make the point that our congregations are formed by their confrontation with the Bible. He says Scripture *forms us*, *reforms us*, and *challenges us*, even as we hide from that Word, refuse to hear it, and avoid and evade the claims it makes upon us.[1] And, indeed, he is right. It has been the testimony of the Bible as the living Word of God that has enabled a people who were no people to gather as God's people around the Word and the sacraments, suggested by the Bible's reports of God's entrance into human affairs.

Show me a vital and healthy congregation, and I will point you to a people who take the Word of God seriously. A congregation that reads it, studies it, listens to God's whispers and shouts in it will be a changed congregation. I found that out for myself in my own experience.

In chapter one I noted that the church I am now pastoring was going through what we all decided was a "spiritual crisis." I asked our congregation to come together to make an assessment, and we began to set some goals for our church. Given the nature of the "spiritual crisis" that prompted our gathering, I was not surprised when we all agreed that our number one goal was "to deepen the spiritual life of our congregation."

I noted that the goal was very broad, and asked by what means we should attempt to reach it. After much thought and discussion, we agreed that we would seek to deepen the spiritual life of the congregation by engaging each member in a serious encounter with the Bible.

This, of course, came as no real surprise to a church in the black tradition. From the earliest days of slavery, the Bible has played an unusually important role in the black church and family. The reverence that they had for the Bible led many ex-slaves, after emancipation, to flock to schools set up by missionaries and other agencies. Carter G. Woodson, the great black historian, observed many years ago: "Negroes almost worshiped the Bible, and their anxiety to read it was their greatest incentive to learn."

One freedman who visited a night school for emancipated slaves in Beaufort, North Carolina, tells the story of a black woman who carried a big Bible with her through the swamps and the woods. Though she was unable to read, she "had got her old mistress to turn down the leaves at the verses she knew by heart, and often she would sit down in the woods and open the big Bible at these verses, and repeat them aloud, and find strength and consolation."[2]

Encountering the name of Jesus in the Bible seemed to have always been important. Woodson tells the story of one slave, who was a nurse for her master's family, who had been taught by one of the children to spell the name of Jesus and to recognize it in the text. It became her devotion to take the Bible and search for the name, but "since she had no idea in what parts of the Bible it was found, she would open the Bible at random and travel with her finger along line after line, and page after page" until she found "Jesus."[3] So it was out of this long background and understanding that we were acting and, in some sense, recapturing.

To facilitate our encounter with the Bible, I made the decision to begin preaching from the New Common Lectionary with the understanding that lectionary study groups would be formed among the members of the congregation throughout the community.

A demographic study showed that our members lived in 80 percent of the voting precincts of Dallas County. To make the Bible study groups accessible to all the members of the congregation, groups were formed throughout the city. They were encouraged to invite nonmembers to join them in their study, thus providing an evangelistic thrust. It is significant that many new members have joined the church after first engaging in Bible study. Indeed, they encountered Jesus in the Bible.

To prepare our leaders of the Bible study groups, discussion guidelines developed by Dr. Richard Murray were used, and he himself participated in the initial training program for the group leaders.

Prior to this time, I had very much opposed lectionary

preaching. I had used simply my own pet texts—which were limited, very limited—and my favorite themes. Not only was I limiting my own encounter with Jesus in the Bible, I was depriving my congregation of the fullness offered by a systematic approach to the multiple themes of the Bible and the faith. In fact, I was team teaching a course in preaching with my colleague Virgil Howard at Perkins School of Theology, where we gave two standard lectures on the Lectionary each year. He gave a lecture on the advantages of preaching from the Lectionary. And I, of course, gave the lecture on the disadvantages of preaching from the Lectionary! My standard line was: "Lectionary preaching robs the freedom of the Holy Spirit to move in the selection of sermon texts."

However, in my search to find a Bible study program, I decided to try a study of the Common Lectionary texts, and to preach from the lections the following Sunday. But even then, I vowed not to become a slave to it. But since I have started using it, to my surprise, not once have I been moved by the Holy Spirit to stray from it! I have always been inspired by one of the texts. Even on special Sundays, such as Martin Luther King Sunday, I have found a word there to move me to preach the lections—even the so-called hard texts.

The Bible study groups studied all four lections each week in preparation for interacting with the sermon on the following Sunday. We also decided to request our members to bring their Bibles to church with them, so that they could follow the Scripture readings and have them ready for reference during the sermon. It was this decision that led me to discover that many of our members did not own Bibles. In other words, many of our members were biblically illiterate, even though they had a profound respect for the authority of the Bible. I began to understand why some of them were so easily attracted to some of the independent Bible churches in which the preacher preached with Bible in hand, even though in some instances the Bible was preached unbiblically! However, this practice gave the impression the preacher was "preaching the Bible."

This realization encouraged us to initiate a program to sell Bibles each Sunday, thus making it convenient for our members to own their personal Bible. Indeed, we sometimes have a friendly "Bible check" in which members are asked to lift up their Bibles during worship.

But more important, the times of Bible study have become occasions for our members and others to encounter Jesus through serious Bible study. For example, during each of our worship services, an invitation to Christian discipleship is extended for members and nonmembers alike. Many of those who respond indicate that their decision was initiated upon their encounter with Jesus in the Bible study groups. In fact, a signal is given to me and the church as members of a Bible study group come forth to surround the person from their group who has responded.

As a result of the Bible study program, we have a much more vital and faithful congregation. All elected officers are required to participate. All outreach programs are motivated and undergirded by a biblical mandate. A new dialogue around the Word of God is frequently the subject of church conversations. All church meetings are preceded by a devotion that is based upon the lectionary readings of the week. Group leaders meet for three hours for continued training once a month. New Bible study programs such as the Disciple Bible Study Program from The United Methodist Publishing House have been launched for persons who desire further study. The psalm of the week has become the basis for a Prayer and Praise Service each Wednesday. A new conversation takes place on Sundays after the sermon is preached. Instead of the usual statements such as "I enjoyed the sermon," I am more likely to get questions and comments that lead to serious dialogue about the meaning of the sermon. Furthermore, I am challenged to preach on questions and comments that flow out of the life of the congregation. And all of this has led me into a deeper encounter with Jesus through my interaction with the Bible study groups, as well as my own study of the Bible. I am no longer avoiding some of the "hard" texts. Because my congregation has had the courage to study them, they expect me to have the courage to preach them.

Whenever I attend a Bible study group, I am amazed to discover that no matter what Scripture reading is being discussed, the members of the group are always able to touch upon every major exegetical and theological issue, even though they have not had any formal biblical or theological training, which confirms my conviction that the Bible is the church's book meant to be studied with other people. Indeed the Word comes alive when the congregation gathers around it, thus enabling the congregation to become vital and faithful.

When I participate with a group I always get feedback that guides me forward in the sermon. I vividly recall a discussion of Elijah's experience on top of Mt. Horeb (I Kings 19:9-12). One member of the group was relating the fact that as Elijah stood on the Mount, the Lord passed by. But the Lord was not in the wind, the earthquake, or the fire; but in a still, small voice. The group member was making the point that the wind, earthquake, and fire were not important; only the still, small voice. However, a twelve-year-old youth in the group said, "The Lord may not have spoken through the wind, earthquake, and fire, but they were important because the Lord used them to get Elijah's attention so that he was ready to listen to the still, small voice." I used that comment in the sermon on the following Sunday, and the people responded with great enthusiasm.

On the other hand, what Martin E. Marty wrote in an article in *The Christian Century* must also be taken seriously:

Emerging today, however, are generations that are tone-deaf to faith's serious demands and rich promises. Even to raise the subject at all, and let people know you are talking about something serious, has become difficult. To talk of faith among the late-stage secular-pluralist contemporaries is like speaking Korean to Armenians or using sign language on the blind.[4]

While his observation certainly describes much of what we face, I believe that even with late-stage secular-pluralist contemporaries, the Bible and the

Jesus of the Bible can be presented in such a way that people can encounter Jesus—and not simply as "a warm tingle in the toes." As difficult as it may be, to enable those who are tone-deaf to hear God's symphonic overtures in Jesus, we must still call his name and still cry out, "Hear him, ye deaf; his praise, ye dumb, your loosened tongues employ; ye blind, behold your Savior come, and leap, ye lame, for joy." It can help us name our pain and sign our way into a new reality. It can help a generation that has looked for happiness, satisfaction, direction, and pleasure in the wrong places find its way back to God. It can help provide an encounter with Jesus in the Bible's story: a covenant with a people, the prophets reminding the people, "and in the fullness of time . . . " We can encounter Jesus, who may not answer all of our questions, but who surely questions all of our answers that do not include his way, his truth, and his life. It is about a God who draws straight with crooked lines and keeps a seat reserved at the table for those who have not yet found their way back home. And that is the gospel truth!

# Encountering Jesus in Worship

S how me a vital congregation and I will point you to a church that gives faithful attention to its worship. And there is no litmus test for the degree of liturgy. Many churches that experience vitality, faithfulness, and growth are churches that have a high degree of liturgy, and others have hardly any fixed liturgy at all. (And I don't mean by "growth" just number: I often make the distinction to my congregation between "growing" and "swelling." One is a sign of health, and one is a clear sign of illness) Perhaps there are tests of the degree of congregational participation; the extent to which the Bible is used as source book, study book, and a book of enrichment; and the uses of music are, in fact, praise to God rather than a rehearsal for a concert hall performance.

My former colleague at Perkins, James F. White, probably one of the best in the business on worship, has observed in an article in *Pulpit Digest*, appropriately titled "Christian Worship in the 1990s," that no one visiting these churches [so-called evangelical churches] can fail to be impressed by the importance of preaching in worship. . . . In some churches, the whole congregation participates vigorously in response to preaching so that it becomes almost dialogue. After visiting various black and Pentecostal churches, I sometimes wonder if other churches know what *participation* really means.

Well, I'm not sure that they do. But one thing my experience has taught me is that you have to bring something to the sermon to get something out of it. The expression is familiar in the African American church: "If you don't put anything in, you won't get anything out!" And sometimes it is a mere openness to the Spirit. For worship is neither something that the clergy does and the people sit back and watch nor something that is an optional activity for the people. Worship is work—hard, active, disciplined, and sometimes painful work that demands something from us as it gives something to us. That is literally what the word that the New Testament uses so often for worship, *leitourgia*, means—"the work of the people." This reminds me of the story of a young college student who returned home for the holidays and accompanied his mother to church one Sunday. After they returned home the young man said, "The preacher was not too good today." His mother said, "Well, maybe not." He said, "I noticed that the choir was not too good today." His mother said, "Well, maybe not." Then she said to him, "Well, son, tell me, how good were *you* today?"

Father Clarence Rivers, a black Roman Catholic

priest and expert in liturgy, has made the observation: "I have never heard a black church minister exhort his congregation to turn out for some particular religious celebration when he did not promise: 'We are going to have a good time!' "[1]

As a matter of fact, "having a good time" is so much characteristic of the authentic black worship experience that the phrase "to have church" has become synonymous with "to have a good time."[2] It even carries over into the funeral service. I asked one of my members how the funeral service of her nephew had gone, since I was not able to attend the service. She replied: "It was a good funeral; we had a good time!" What she was saying was that the service was a celebration, that "they had church!"

This approach of celebration and festive worship does not deny the seriousness of worship. It is joy in the midst of sorrow. It is hope in the very depths of despair. It is a way of saying with Charles Albert Tindley: "I believe it. I believe it. Jesus died to set me free!" It is an affirmation of the words of Jesus: "In the world you face persecution. But take courage; I have conquered the world!" (John 16:33). And every pastor ought to know that every Sunday is a season of the gospel, and every occasion of gathering is an opportunity to say with the church and the Christ of the church: "Come to me, all of you who are heavy laden," all of you who desire purpose and meaning, all of you who have lost hope, all of you who need rest, all of you who seek, Come!

I have been pleased to see the emphasis of congregational participation in the liturgical renewal movement in The United Methodist Church. The new

Service of Death and Resurrection, officially adopted by
the 1984 General Conference and now a part of the new
*United Methodist Hymnal,* reflects this. It is a service of
Christian worship suitable for funerals and memorial
services in which the congregation actively participates.
This is a great improvement over the clergy-dominated
earlier service where, if you wanted any extensive
congregational participation, a bulletin had to be
printed. It is more than an improvement, it is
recapturing what is so essential to vital worship that is
faithful to the church's beginnings.

But congregational participation alone does not make
worship necessarily Christian worship. And not all
worship done within the so-called "Christian community" is Christian, in spite of the celebrative spirit. It can
sometimes be mere self-worship or ego trips or worship
of something or somebody who is not the Holy One. As
H. Grady Davis was so fond of saying: "The worship of
the pagan is a *search,* but the worship of a Christian is
*recognition.''* What, then, makes worship Christian?

First, it is Christian worship when it is our response to
God's initiative in addressing us and inviting us through
Jesus Christ. In other words, it is not something we do.
It begins with something God has already done through
Jesus Christ. Our worship is in response to a gracious
invitation that has been extended through Jesus Christ.
At least part of what this means is that we don't come
to worship to find God. We come to be found by God or
to acknowledge we have already been found by God and
to encounter Jesus. Really, we come because we have
heard of or know of a God who is seeking us, as a
shepherd who goes hunting for a sheep, as a woman who

sweeps the floor of a candle-lit room to find a lost coin, as a father who takes the initiative to greet a lost son who has returned home; even before he gets all the way to the porch, the father is saying, "That's my boy who I've been waiting for. Let's have a celebration." And that same God is our God or can be our God.

Second, it is Christian worship when it is an upward look, a recognition and adoration of God. In the classic passage in the sixth chapter of Isaiah we note that, according to the prophet's own words, the service begins with an *overpowering awareness* of the presence and the majesty of God. He said:

> I saw the Lord sitting on a throne, high and lofty; and the hem of his robe filled the temple. Seraphs were in attendance above him; each had six wings: with two they covered their faces, and with two they covered their feet, and with two they flew. And one called to another and said:
> "Holy, Holy, Holy is the LORD of hosts;
> the whole earth is full of his glory." (Isaiah 6:1-3)

Worship is, in a real sense, a response of praise. We gather and respond in acts of praise and adoration.

In the third place, Christian worship involves an inward look. The moment I look up to God I also recognize myself for what I am. After Isaiah saw the glory of the Lord, he realized how far short he had fallen from the glory of God. So after an inward look he cries out: "Woe is me! I am lost, for I am a man of unclean lips, and I live among a people of unclean lips" (Isaiah 6:5). Here it is important to note that he *recognized* and

*confessed* his own uncleanliness before he acknowledged the uncleanliness of other people.

It is an act that corresponds to the teaching of Jesus in
the Sermon on the Mount. Jesus said:

> "Why do you see the speck in your neighbor's eye, but
> do not notice the log in your own eye? Or how can you
> say to your neighbor, 'Let me take the speck out of your
> eye,' while the log is in your own eye? You hypocrite,
> first take the log out of your own eye and then you will
> see clearly to take the speck out of your neighbor's eye."
> (Matthew 7:3-5; see also Luke 6:41-42)

Isaiah's act of acknowledging the corporate nature of sin
as well as personal sin also reminds us of the corporate
nature of worship. A distinguishing characteristic of
Christian worship is that it is never a solitary undertaking.
Instead, it is thoroughly social and organic in character.
Jesus said, "Where two or three are gathered in my name,
I am there among them" (Matthew 18:20). This does not
negate the fact that common worship ought to be
supplemented with private devotion. But the distinction
needs to be clear. Both need to take place—*common
worship* where there is the physical presence of the rest of
the Body of Christ and *personal devotion*, which usually
occurs apart from the gathered community. There needs
to be a balance of each.

After Isaiah confessed his sins and acknowledged the
corporate nature of sin and worship, he experienced the
forgiveness of God. He said: "Then one of the seraphs
flew to me, holding a live coal that had been taken from
the altar with a pair of tongs. The seraph touched my

mouth with it and said: 'Now that this has touched your lips, your guilt has departed and your sin is blotted out" (Isaiah 6:6-7). The uniqueness of this act in Christian worship is that it comes through Jesus Christ, our liberator, who is at the center of all that happens. Christian worship is encountering Jesus.

Christian worship must also have an outward look. After Isaiah's sins are forgiven, he said that he heard the voice saying to him: "Whom shall I send, and who will go for us?" Then Isaiah answers: "Here am I; send me!" (Isaiah 6:8). And God said: "Go!" Thus Christian worship is a come and go affair.

In worship Jesus extends a gracious invitation for us to come to him, he wants us to rest. He wants us to learn of him. But he also wants us to go for him. He not only wants us to be the *gathered church,* he also wants us to be the *church scattered.*

There is the classic occasion in the Gospels that illustrates the challenge of this truth. It is usually called "The Transformation." Jesus took Peter, James, and John, and went to the top of a mountain, where Jesus was transformed before them. Jesus talked with Moses and Elijah. Peter became so captivated by it all that he said: "Lord, we are having such a good time, let's stay here! Let's build three booths and stay here forever! Let's freeze time. Let's eternalize this moment." But Jesus said to Peter: "No, Peter, we didn't come up here to stay. This is a *come and go affair.* We have come up, but we must go down. There is a distraught father in the valley who needs help. A sick boy needs healing. There is a woman who has been hemorrhaging for twelve years and needs healing. There is an unbelieving, stumbling, and fumbling church that needs better organization. Let's go down."

In this regard, the Puritans had the right idea. They did not apply the word "service" to the gathering of worship. For them the _service_ began at the church door when the church meeting was over. There they crossed the threshold of life to go back into the world, and there the service began as an outgrowth of the renewal that had come as they worshiped together. Worship loses its essential Christian nature when it becomes an end in itself and does not send its worshipers out into the world to engage in Christian service, to deal with the problems of the poor and the oppressed.

The Jesus who invites us to worship is the same Jesus who proclaimed in his first sermon, as recorded in Luke 4:18-19:

"The Spirit of the Lord is upon me,
    because he has anointed me to bring good news to the
        poor.
He has sent me to proclaim release to the captives
    and recovery of sight to the blind,
        to let the oppressed go free,
to proclaim the year of the Lord's favor."

James Cone has often made the point that in black worship there is a sense of what he calls "the eschatological community." This is found in the belief of the people that the Spirit of Jesus is coming to visit with them in the worship or what I have continued to refer to in this chapter as "encountering Jesus in worship."

This presence of the Holy Spirit is a liberating

experience from complete control of the ritual. Ritual is important, but it is not an end in itself. Ritual is interrupted freely when the Spirit moves. The clock is not worshiped. The preacher is told by the congregation, "Take your time!" And if he or she is saying something, the people will stay and listen, for part of what happens when the Spirit visits is a radical transformation in the people's identity. Those who were no people become God's people. Those who have thought of themselves as nobody become somebody. You can see it in their walk. You can hear it in their talk. And if you give them a chance, they will tell the story of how an encounter with Jesus enabled them to overcome their lack of identities!

Where worship is vital and faithful, and this is certainly not confined to black and Pentecostal churches, several elements must be present. The first is celebration—that is, a sense that life and the gathering itself are pure gift. Praise to God and acknowledgment to God for God's gracious gifts and acts of grace are necessary. Surely Christians who "gather in his name" have even more to celebrate or at least ought to be aware of more for which to give thanksgiving and praise than those who gather at our weekly fall and winter secular celebration—the American football game. And yet one sees much more enthusiasm and joy expressed at these gatherings than most of our weekly worship services. Can it be that these secular gatherings tend to be simple, aggressive, direct? Frank C. Senn thinks so and writes in his book *Christian Worship and Its Cultural Setting* that "celebrations must make an impression on those who participate in them if what cult communicates is nothing less than reality itself—a worldview and life-style that is intended to be shared by all members of the society."[3]

A second element is inclusiveness. The makeup of the congregation ought to reflect the makeup of the community and a hearty welcome should be extended to everyone. Historically, it was not unusual in the black congregation to include both the poorest of the poor and the wealthiest African Americans in the community. The educated and the uneducated sat side by side. Congregations were intergenerational; children and youth and young adults and middle-aged and the elderly were all present together. The very nature of such a diverse congregation demanded that the service have something for everyone, that all the sheep be fed. I suspect where there are vital and faithful churches that is still true. But one of the greatest threats to the integrity of worship in the African American church is the rising classism among black Christians. There is a widening social gap between upwardly mobile, middle-class blacks and poor blacks. This gap is reflected in the membership of many black churches today. My heart aches as I see this develop. A common expression of the early black churches was that the ground is level at the foot of the cross. Our challenge is to recover this notion in all our churches today. The invitation Jesus issued was to all. There are some invitations we do not receive because we do not necessarily meet the criteria or the standards or don't have the credentials or we would be out of place. But not so with the church. The invitation goes out to all: "Whosoever will, let them come." The old Charles Wesley hymn captured Jesus' invitation well. It is worth looking at every word to remind us, and especially *all* Methodists, of our good beginnings:

> Come, sinners, to the gospel feast;
> Let every soul be Jesus' guest.
> Ye need not one be left behind,
> For God hath bid all humankind.
>
> Sent by my Lord, on you I call;
> The invitation is to all.
> Come, all the world! Come, sinner, thou!
> All things in Christ are ready now.
>
> Come, all ye souls by sin oppressed,
> Ye restless wanderers after rest;
> Ye poor, and maimed, and halt, and blind,
> In Christ a hearty welcome find.
>
> My message as from God receive;
> Ye all may come to Christ land live.
> O let his love your hearts constrain,
> Nor suffer him to die in vain.
>
> This is the time, no more delay!
> This is the Lord's accepted day;
> Come thou this moment, at his call,
> And live for him who died for all.[4]

A third element is an understanding of Scripture from the perspective of the underside. Both in preaching and teaching we must draw freely from the Old and New Testaments. The Christian church is a two-testament church. We cannot and shall not forget the Exodus theme: "Let my people go!" even as we hear the

Resurrection story and live out a Resurrection faith. The
Old Testament prophets denounced social injustices
and called for "justice to roll down like waters and
righteousness like an ever flowing stream." In preaching, it means interpreting the Scripture story of David
by not identifying with David the king, but by helping
the people to identify with David the shepherd boy who,
though he was an underdog, overcame the giant,
Goliath, with a sling shot and a few stones. It is
preaching that identifies with the wounded, and not
with the Levite and the priest in the story of the good
Samaritan. It is preaching that identifies with a Christ
who was born in a stable instead of a luxurious inn! It is
preaching that finds the liberating activity of Jesus as a
clue for understanding our life and ministry. Not only do
we understand the Resurrection event as victory over
sin and death, but also as the power to overcome
oppressive and unjust conditions. And the challenge to
see both Good Friday and Easter Sunday must be
present in our proclamation of the faith. There can be no
Resurrection without the Crucifixion.

We have discussed earlier the role of the Bible in the
black church. What also must be added here is that we
are not merely talking about a fundamentalist, proof-
texting, uncritical, and unthinking use of the Bible. We
are talking about a reverence for the Scriptures as
authority, a confronting as well as comforting word, and
a realization that the Book has been a real source of oral
tradition that is inherently embedded in our lives and
our culture. This understanding has given a certain
freedom of interpretation that is perhaps absent in many
other church circles. It is clearly present in the way the

black preacher can take an ancient text like that of the good Samaritan or the prodigal son or the story of the Hebrew men in the fiery furnace and make it live in twentieth-century America.[5]

To be sure, one of the greatest challenges for the whole church in the twentieth century is to rediscover the Bible as our authority and guide for faithful discipleship. The challenge was underscored by pollster George Gallup, Jr., at a recent convention of the Evangelical Press Association. He noted that most Americans say they believe in God and Jesus and trust the Bible. "However, statistics show that Americans are ignorant of the doctrines and history of their chosen faiths, and half of the nation's Christians do not know who delivered the sermon on the mount," he said. "We revere the Bible, but don't read it," he continued. "We believe the Ten Commandments to be valid rules for living, although we can't name them."

A fourth element in Worship is Music. I have always felt that the music of the church ought to be diverse. That has not always been true of the congregations I have served. It was only after I was able to work on the advisory committee that produced *Songs of Zion*, a book containing spirituals and gospel songs as well as hymns and anthem arrangements, that I was able to convince my congregation that a variety of music in worship was acceptable. It is a treasured resource now in our worship. And I gladly welcomed the chance to sit on the national advisory committee to produce *Come Sunday* (the companion to *Songs of Zion*) by William B. McClain. It helps us integrate liturgy and music so that every service can reflect the inclusiveness and diversity I spoke of earlier.

But after all is said and done about worship, there is only one criterion for Christian worship: gathering in Jesus' name. It is recorded in the Gospel of Matthew 18:20: "For where two or three are gathered in my name, I am there among them." Whether the gathering together is in a rural clapboard building or in an urban Gothic cathedral; whether there are three thousand, three hundred or just two or three, the criterion is the same: to gather in Jesus' name. Christians gather in worship around the Word and the Table to speak and touch in Christ's name, and the promise in the New Testament Gospel is that he will be present.

In an age when so many are lonely and seek companionship and friendly groups to be with or to join just to avoid boredom or merely being alone, the church must be clear that the purpose of its worship is to gather in Christ's name, to encounter Jesus, the Holy One, and to call his name, praise his name, and to be encountered by him in prayer and praise and preaching. So many congregations fail to experience genuine worship and spend much time in solemn assembly or in extra efforts to create the friendly atmosphere and "tingly feelings" because they forget the purpose for gathering.

Added to the problem is the unfortunate notion that if people look alike, think alike, talk alike, dress alike, and have about the same amounts in their bank accounts, they can huddle together and sing a few songs and read a few prayers and listen to a talk on a religious subject, and then they have worshiped. Such gatherings are much more numerous than we at first want to admit. This is at least a part of our problem as we struggle to understand why so many congregations are neither vital nor faithful.

There can be no vital congregation without people who intentionally gather to encounter Jesus—even in those old and familiar places where, in the past, perhaps perverted gatherings have replaced the authentic worship of the people of God.

Vital and faithful worship is necessary and sufficient condition for building vital and faithful congregations. While the forms and styles may be diverse, the musical genres varied, the degree of liturgy different in quantity and kind, the Word preached and read in different ways and languages, the questions become: Was there a rehearsal of the gracious acts of God in the past, the present, and the promise for the future? Was there an encounter with a Holy God? Was there a sense that we are the created and a people prone to dip into the social swine pen of life and stay to live as if we are not those who are called to be God's people? Was there a reminder that we owe thanks and praise to the one from whom all blessings have come? Did we say, "Much obliged!" Did we show gratitude for goodness and grace? Was there a reminder of our obligation to act and care about those people and things that the Grace-giver cares about? Did we encounter Jesus in his risen power?

# Encountering Jesus in Preaching

W hat is so often lost in our effort to preach is the role of the congregation in the preaching task. In so many instances the preacher sees it as a solo performance. Part of this has to do with an understanding of preaching as the *primary* task of the pastor.

What I am proposing is the model of the preaching congregation as a means of facilitating an encounter with Jesus through the sermon. Such a model can help develop a vital and faithful congregation.

While the importance of proclaiming the Word cannot be neglected, nay, must not be—"lest the rocks cry out!"—preaching is the cooperative effort of the pulpit and the pew. What P. T. Forsyth suggested long ago is still a word to us all: "The one great preacher in history is the church. And the first business of the individual preacher is to enable the church to preach."[1]

I shall never forget the year 1959. That was the year I was graduated from seminary. That was also the year I realized a life-long dream—to become the pastor of a local church.

When I arrived at Hamilton Park United Methodist Church in Dallas, Texas, with seminary degree in hand, I was excited and anxious about many things. I was most particularly excited about the task of preaching. To be sure, I had learned in seminary that *all* of the functions of ministry were important for effective and competent ministry. And I believed that. But I had also learned from my experience in the black church that the first thing the black congregation asks about its pastor is, Can the reverend tell the story?

Indeed, this emphasis upon preaching was further reinforced in my very being by the oft-repeated admonition of some of my preaching elders who said, "If preaching is not your main business, then you have no business preaching."

Now I am certain that the congregation and the preaching elders in this particular tradition did not disparage the need for the pastor to be competent and proficient in the other functions of ministry. But their stated emphasis led me to believe that if I did not demonstrate *immediate* effectiveness in preaching, I would not be around long enough to demonstrate my competence in the other functions of ministry.

Later on in my ministry I became the district superintendent of a predominantly white district. And, after meeting with numerous pastor-parish relations committees, I learned that effective preaching is a major concern of most congregations. This was further underscored with lay committees during my years with the Perkins School of Theology school intern program.

In the meantime, back at Hamilton Park in 1959, I began my preaching ministry with an understanding of preaching that led me to believe that it was a *solo performance* by the pastor. This understanding was augmented by a parish situation that suggested that I do much of my work alone. I did not have to consult with other staff members. I *was* the staff! Most of my congregation worked during the day, so I had very limited contact with them, except during evening hours and weekends. Even in those congregations where staff and congregation are available, there are ministerial duties that are usually done alone (such as hospital calls, study time, and acts of administration). So I accommodated to a style of ministry in which I was often alone.

I began to understand why the ministry is often depicted as a lonely profession. Sometimes lay people set us apart and keep us isolated. But often this is our own doing. Too often we try to carry the whole burden of ministry by ourselves. We forget that the ministry belongs to the whole church. We forget that to be baptized in the church is to be called into the ministry of the church.

On Mondays when I started the process of sermon preparation I asked the perennial question that is asked by most preachers: "On what shall I preach next Sunday?" At that time I was out of touch with the "exegesis" of this question that is provided in an article by Thomas Troeger, then professor of preaching at Colgate-Rochester Divinity School. He says:

> First, it assumes that only "I" am preaching. Second, the form of the verb, "preach on," suggests that a

sermon is a pronouncement on some topic. The preacher will speak on love in the same way the president speaks on the economy or a teacher lectures *on* history. Finally, the questions relate the sermon to only one point in time, Sunday. Thus the question implies that preaching is the act of a solitary self speaking on an isolated topic at a singular point in time. There is no hint that the Word that needs to be spoken may already be circulating in the listeners' lives.[2]

As I look back on my sermons from that period I find that they included much abstract language, very few concrete examples, and had a tone of explanation rather than invitation to have an encounter with Jesus. I revealed more about Barth, Tillich, Niebuhr, and Bultmann than I did about either myself or the Savior. To be honest, I did not want to reveal much of myself to my congregation for fear my congregation would discern that I, too, was just as human as they were and standing in the same need.

I also discovered that my sermons of that period were undergirded by an approach to the Bible that Justo and Catherine Gonzalez characterize as a "Lone Ranger Bible Study Syndrome."[3] In this approach there is an excessive emphasis upon private Bible study to the neglect of corporate or group study. And even when the value of both forms of Bible study are acknowledged, the Lone Ranger Syndrome dictates that private study is somehow better or deeper or more meaningful.

My biblical exegesis failed to take into account that "most of the Bible was written to be read, not in private, but in public, often within the context of corporate worship."[4] According to the Gonzalezes, the Lone

Ranger did not roam the West alone. He had Tonto with him. But in spite of this, the hero was called "lone" because his Indian companion (who repeatedly saved his life) simply did not count.

They note that "this (also) happens when our biblical interpretation fails to be challenged by others, either because they share our own perspective, or because, since they differ from us, we classify them as 'Tontos' whose perspectives we need not take into account."[5]

In my early years of preaching and Bible study, lay people were my "Tontos." They repeatedly saved my life, but I did not listen to them, for at this time they did not count in the preaching process. Also, my preaching particularly suffered during these years because it was undergirded by an understanding of *practical theology* that emphasized the application of doctrine *to* life rather than the discovery of doctrine *in* life.

During my first year at Hamilton Park, I considered myself to be the authority on all matters of doctrine and life. After all, I had earned a degree from Perkins School of Theology! I had the vital information, and it was my responsibility to provide it for the less fortunate and deprived members of my congregation. Thus I understood my task as preacher to apply matters of doctrine and life to those who were unaware of such issues. Unintentionally, I was using a "banking concept" of education that has been coined by Paulo Friere. That concept says that the teacher has all the information, which is *deposited* in the student's mind, the receptacle. The student is expected to receive the information as given and feed it back to the teacher who gives a premium grade to that which comes back unaltered.

I had a banking concept of preaching. I was *unprepared* to accept the fact that, in so many instances, the members of my congregation knew much more about doctrine and life than I knew. But the longer I was there, the more I came to the realization that I was not telling them what they did not know. Instead, I was only identifying something that God had already done through them. They may not have been able to articulate it in the terms that I used, but they knew it to be true in their own life experiences. An example of this was related by one of my students in a sermon he preached at Perkins. He told of the experience of a young, "turned-on" seminary student who went out to practice his profession. He was determined to find somebody and tell them everything they needed to know about God. He selected as his target area a run-down tenement neighborhood (where else?), and he walked until he found an old man sitting on the curb—a rather rugged-looking individual.

When the young man saw him he said to himself: "Well, if anybody looks like they need to know something about God, this fella does." So the young, "turned-on" seminary student went up to the old man, placed his hand on his shoulder, and said, "Old man, let me tell you about God."

The younger man paused to see how the old man was going to respond. After a long reflective pause, the old man responded with a story. This is the story he told:

My grandfather was a freed-man. But somehow he managed to get hold of a piece of land and build a home on it. My father inherited the land and worked it, but one year our crop was not too good . . . and when the depression came I left home to make it easier for my folks. . . . I survived wandering around . . . selling whatever I could get my hands on. . . . For a while I was drinking real heavy. . . . I got married but it didn't last. . . . I had been in jail more times than I can count. . . . A few days ago they kicked me out of my apartment . . . couldn't pay the rent . . . ain't got nowhere to go . . . folks died about thirty years ago . . . I ain't sure where my brothers and sisters are.

After hearing this, the young man put his hand back on the old man's shoulder and said, "Old man, sounds like you sure need to know about God." The old man raised an eyebrow at him and said: "Young man, what I've been trying to tell you is, I know about God! Who do you think helped me to last this long? How do you think I could have survived without knowing God? Had it not been for the grace of God, I couldn't have made it."

After many similar "discoveries" on my part in the life of the congregation I finally got the point: our task is not to introduce the Word, but to expose the Word that is already there. In the words of Dietrich Ritschl:

> Speaking and hearing belong together, so that there can be no preacher who has not heard the Word and no hearer who can remain silent. Since it is not possible to be a hearer in privacy without the [fellowship] of believers, it must be the intention of all preachers to belong to a circle of members of the church with whom the Word is heard before it is preached. There is no

direct route from the privacy of the study to the pulpit. . . . The office of proclamation belongs to the whole church and not just the preacher.[6]

On the day of Pentecost the Holy Spirit was given not to isolated individuals, but to a worshiping community that faced the world of need together. Therefore, regardless of the preaching tradition in which it is delivered, the faithful sermon is always a mutual undertaking between pulpit and pew.

## The Preaching Congregation

The cooperative effort of preaching sometimes involved a preaching congregation and a listening preacher. Henry Mitchell says it well when he writes:

> Preaching cannot be the private province of an elite priesthood, even though that professional body must do much to make the word/experience worthy of the title Gospel. Persons learn and grow because of involvement far better than they do from detachment and inert attention. Ritual and other forms of dialogue offer much in this vein toward the recovery of preaching.[7]

Reuel Howe makes a similar point about the general ministry of the church, including the preaching ministry. He asserts,

> The theology of ministry implicit in the kind of preaching in which the preacher is solely responsible contradicts the doctrine of ministry that we profess. We profess that all ministries are the ministry of the

Church, and since the Church is made up of clergy and laity, it follows that both have responsibilities in all ministries, and this is no less true for preaching.[8]

It follows that if the pastor is to truly become the preaching pastor, he or she must first of all become the listening pastor to hear what the preaching congregation has to say. Now, unfortunately, the art of listening is one that has almost disappeared in our noisy and busy day. Someone has said that ours is the "Age of the Unfinished Sentence." Usually when we are engaged in conversation, we are so eager to make our comments or insert our opinions that as soon as the next person pauses for breath we leap in as if we are driven by some kind of compulsive vocal disease! I imagine that when we master the art of speaking while inhaling, conversation will cease altogether! I have a friend who says that God evidently intended for us to do twice as much listening as we do talking because we were given two ears but only one mouth!

But there *are* times when the listening of the preacher is more important than the preacher's talking. As a listener, the preacher becomes aware to what extent the congregation is a witnessing community with a story to tell and, therefore, a preaching congregation. When properly encouraged and employed, the resources of members of the congregation can be a lift to the preacher rather then a put-down.

I recall hearing the late Bishop Paul Martin tell of the time when he received a new church appointment early in his ministry. The congregation planned a reception for him on his first Sunday. During the reception everyone came around to greet him except for one man who lingered in the rear of the room. After everyone else had greeted him, this man came forward and simply stood there. The future bishop asked him, "What do you do here?" The layman said, "I look for the preacher's weaknesses." And he added, "I'm good at it! But when I find them, that's where I get beneath him, and then I lift him up."

Now, there are several vital and important areas in which the preaching congregation shares a witness that can give a lift to preaching in the church today.

First, the preaching congregations help to uplift the preaching of the preacher *before* the sermon is preached if the preacher will view the congregation "not as an audience but as the Community through whose life the sermon has been born."[9]

For example, I found this approach to preaching to be extremely uplifting in the development of the funeral sermon. I recall that during the early years of my preaching, I had great difficulty preaching funeral sermons. This was created in part by my own uneasiness regarding the issue of death, but it was also caused by the fact that often I felt that in order to be effective I had to remove myself from the family of the deceased to some silent sanctuary. There I engaged in a solo flight and eventually landed upon what I considered to be some appropriate and relevant word. Almost always I was never satisfied with the results. Then one day I was invited by a dear saint, along with her family, to share her funeral plans prior to her death. As she and her family members shared their favorite scriptures, hymns, and faith experiences, a powerful and appropriate sermon idea came alive that was liberating, comforting, and faith-affirming.

Through such a sharing process of sermon development, I became more comfortable, relevant, and faithful with the funeral sermon. Also, it is my experience that the process increases, rather than decreases, the authority of the pulpit, because the sermon is supported and reinforced by the witness and experience of the preaching congregation, as represented by the family members.

A variation on this process of sermon development is the piano player in cult churches who picks up the melody according to the key of the singing congregation, thus reversing the practice in the mainline churches where the instrument first gives the key, and the singers follow. A careful listening to the melody of the preaching congregation, as well as the melody of the biblical Word, assures that preaching is done in the right way.

Some years ago, according to John D. Godsey, Karl Barth observed that "any Christian who wishes to live responsibly must read two things: the Bible and the daily newspaper—and never the one without the other!"[16] Likewise, the responsible preacher listens to two texts: the biblical text and the contextual or situational text, which includes, of course, the preaching congregation.

Sandy Ray, the late great preaching pastor of the Cornerstone Baptist Church of Brooklyn, New York, compared the preparation of sermons to the wife who goes to the supermarket for good nutrition, and she also has her own imagination. But she always has her family in mind. They determine what she selects. So likewise, he suggests, that preachers are shopping all the time—and if we are to touch home base we must keep the interests and needs of our congregations in mind.

A classical biblical example of how the preaching congregation helps to uplift the preaching of the congregation is the experience of the prophet Ezekiel. His congregation was a congregation that was languishing in captivity. Describing his relationship with them, Ezekiel says: "I came to the exiles at Tel-a-bib, who lived by the river Chebar. And I sat there among them, stunned, for seven days" (Ezekiel 3:15). Commenting on this passage, Henry Mitchell shares the following insights, which support the value of the preaching congregation:

> During the vision early in his ministry, one gets the feeling that people were busy tuning Ezekiel out—that nobody was listening. But then there is the twenty-third chapter, after Ezekiel began to really sit where they sat, the report is that people said, "Come and listen. Come and hear; this man has something to say that matches our needs. Come and hear this man; he has something to say that relates to us, that we can understand, something that will help us."[11]

Because Ezekiel engaged in a dialogic process that attuned him to the witness of his congregation, he was able to communicate both an appropriate and relevant Word.

Ezekiel's experience also illustrates the fact that the biblical prophet was never a "visiting fireman." Instead, the prophets always arose out of their own communities and were nourished by their self-understanding and witness. Likewise, the witness of our congregations can provide rich nourishment to the preaching task *before* the sermon is preached.

Second, the preaching congregation can help uplift the preaching of the preacher *after* the sermon has been proclaimed in the worship service. For example, the congregation can function as a helpful evaluation-feedback mechanism to the minister. When used properly, such a feedback mechanism can lead the preacher forward to increased effectiveness in the pulpit. In reality, preachers have no choice of whether or not to employ the congregation as an evaluation feedback mechanism. They are constantly being evaluated and offered feedback, whether it is solicited or not. The preacher only has the choice of getting evaluation formally and structured or informally and unstructured.

I know one preacher who says that he gets informal evaluation feedback from an elderly woman as she shakes his hand at the conclusion of every service. He says he has done well if she says, "Reverend, you fed my soul so well I'll have food to last all week long." But he says that when he has not done so well she says, "Reverend, I'll be praying for you all week long."

There are many other informal ways in which the congregation preaches back to the preacher *after* the word has been proclaimed in the worship service. Sometimes it is delayed feedback that may come long after the sermon is proclaimed. Some time ago, I preached a revival in El Paso, Texas. After the first sermon, I was greeted at the door by a man whom I had not seen in ten years. Seeing his wife was not with him, I inquired about her. He informed me that she had chosen to worship at another church. I told him to tell her that I would like to see her before I left town. She responded to my message and was present in the services that evening. At the conclusion of the service, she joyfully expressed surprise that I inquired about her and wanted to see her. She then proceeded to tell me that she had not planned to attend any of the services because she was *turned off* by something she understood me to say in a sermon some ten years ago! I was grateful for the evaluation-feedback, though long delayed. It helped us to resolve an issue of faith and action. But I regret that no evaluation-feedback, informal or otherwise, enabled us to deal with the issue sooner.

It is for this reason and others that many preachers are becoming more intentional in soliciting ways to hear the congregation preach-back *after* the sermon has been proclaimed. Some preachers have organized formal talk-back sessions at various times during the week. Early in my ministry I took advantage of a Sunday evening Bible class I taught to get evaluation-feedback on my morning sermons. We usually spent the first few minutes discussing the sermon. I have found the dialogue to be a challenging and growing experience for both the listening preacher and the preaching congregation.

Also, I have learned not to let my members get by with the casual "I-enjoyed-your-sermon-this-morning" comment. More often than not I now respond by asking: "What specifically did you like about it?" For those who dare to ask the question, it is a good way to hear the congregation preach after the sermon has been proclaimed in the worship service.

In addition to evaluation-feedback, the preaching congregation also shares responsibility for the continued care and delivery of the sermon *after* worship—when it becomes incarnate in their lives. Thomas Troeger tells of a visitor to the studio of Henry Moore, the famous sculptor. Inquiring about a particular piece of work, the visitor asked Moore, "Is this finished?" Moore replied, "None of my work is finished until it is seen and responded to."[12]

So it is with sermons. They are not finished unless they become *incarnate* in the lives of the preaching congregation, which proclaims them in the life of the world. In some sense, we ought to ask the question: Is my preaching portable? Is it repeatable? Can it walk as well as it can talk?

But the more serious test of the sermon is: Did the congregation (and that includes the preacher) encounter Jesus in some way in the proclamation of the gospel? Sometimes we encounter Jesus as the transforming Christ who changes our lives and makes us new creatures, and we say "Yes!" to what God has done for us. Sometimes we encounter Jesus as a healer, a comforter, a friend who heals our brokenness and gives support and guidance for coping with life's demands and wounds. Sometimes we encounter Jesus as the Christ who calls us to vital piety and urges and enables us to move from one degree of grace to another—providing the grace for daily triumphs of grace: "grace upon grace." In the words of the old spiritual, "every round goes higher and higher." Sometimes we encounter him as the Ancient Prophet of Galilee who steps across the centuries still urging and demanding that we seek justice, feed the hungry, find a home that is really home and not merely a shelter for the homeless, give comfort to people with AIDS, and help those who are addicted to drugs, and create a world where there is bread with dignity, peace with justice, liberation with power, and life with wholeness. But always we encounter him as the Presence and the Challenge amidst our pride and glory and our noisy assembly, the Christ of God whose "name is above every name," and at whose name every knee shall bow and every tongue confess him as the King of glory!

Third, the preaching congregation can help uplift the preaching of the preacher *during* the worship service. For me, this is best understood, illustrated, and experienced in the black preaching tradition. While this is not the only way, and I have been in congregations where there is clearly a dialogic experience in preaching, it is my best example. However, I have been amazed and surprised and rewarded in so many places—in Annual Conferences across the church, in convocations, and in local churches—where this has happened. Indeed it has made me feel it is possible for any congregation. In fact, when preaching in predominately white congregations, I often begin by saying, "Let the church say Amen!" The congregation always responds with a verbal amen! One white pastor told me he continued the practice after I left. To his pleasant surprise, his congregation is providing some verbal feedback during the sermon.

But my best example is still the black church and its unique way of responding to the preached Word and the response of the people *during* the sermon. It is characterized by a preaching style that is based upon a pattern of call and response which is deeply rooted and nourished in our African tradition.

The authentic black worship service is a genuine dialogical event in which everyone in the congregation is affirmed and elicited as an important and critical part of the sermon proclamation. While some preachers in other traditions may deliver their sermons as though their congregations do not exist or are not a vitally necessary part of the communication event, for the most part, this practice would seriously damage the effectiveness of the preacher in the black church.

Sandy Ray once told of a conversation he had after a spirited worship service with an attorney who was a member of his congregation. The attorney said: "Reverend Ray, I enjoy your preaching, but those people down front keep up so much noise that I can't hear what you are saying." Sandy Ray replied: "If they weren't keeping up that much noise down front, I wouldn't be saying anything *worth* hearing!"

In the call and response pattern, the black preacher solicits on-the-spot "feedback" and "feed-forward" by asking such questions as "Have I got a witness?" "Are you listening?" "Isn't that right?" or "Are you praying with me?" The congregation responds, "Yes, sir!" "Yes, ma'am!" "Go ahead!" "Come on up!" "Say it!" "A-men!" and "Tell it like it is!"

Above all, the authentic congregation, through the power of the Holy Spirit, functions as a *supportive fellowship* that uses all of its resources to hold the preacher up and keep him or her from failing. I had to learn this the hard way on the occasion of my very first sermon. I was a student in seminary, and I was doing my field work with Dr. I. B. Loud at St. Paul Church. One Sunday morning as we were all standing to sing the hymn of preparation, Dr. Loud turned to me and said: "Okay, son, it's yours this morning!" I was terrified. I had never preached a sermon in my life!

I do not remember how I got to the pulpit, but the Holy Spirit must have gotten me there. I was taking a course in homiletics, and I suddenly remembered that I had started writing a Lenten sermon on the experience of Jesus in the Garden of Gethsemane. Talking about identifying with Jesus, I had no problem whatsoever! I repeated those words of Jesus when he said: "Father, if thou be willing, remove this cup from me!" But God, being God, just as God was with Jesus, refused to move the cup!

So I started out preaching, haunted by the fact that I had not written a conclusion to the sermon. Well, I got as far as I had written and my mind went blank! I just stood there! Talk about "leaning on the everlasting arms." I was leaning on the arms, shoulders, and chest of the Lord. And then it happened. A little old lady stood and said: "He'p him, Jesus!" Then another dear saint of the church said, "Yes, Lord!" Next I heard a male voice from the choir loft saying, "Come, Holy Spirit!" People in the congregation began to moan. Little children sitting on the front pew began to clap their hands. And all of a sudden the entire congregation rose to their feet with shouts of praise and thanksgiving. Through the prompting of the Holy Spirit that preaching congregation provided the conclusion to my sermon. I did not have to say another word. I simply turned around, walked to my seat, and sat down.

Now I think I understand what Søren Kierkegaard meant when he said:

> Many people go to church as they would go to a theatre, expecting to hear a performance by the minister, and to judge how well he does. But in reality, . . . the roles are quite different. In church it is the hearer who is on stage, under the spotlight. The preacher is the prompter who is just off the scene, whispering the lines to the players. If they forget their parts, he is there to remind them. The hearer, out on the stage, is supposed to catch the prompter's lines and work them into his act. The audience who is watching the players and the prompter, and judging how well they do their parts, is Almighty God.[13]

Paul reminds us that "We have this treasure in earthen vessels." However, I am convinced that if we earnestly desire to become listening preachers before a preaching congregation, helping our congregations to encounter Jesus, to see an injured Mother's or Father's face, to experience the God fact, to give a lift to those who have grown weary in the long journey, God's Holy Spirit will bless our efforts and use us for the sake of the proclamation of the gospel. We shall then see the assembly of a vital and faithful congregation gathered around the word that *is* the Word. For this Jesus we preach is in fact the Christ, and the Christ himself is *the* Word!

# Encountering Jesus in the Life of the Church and the Community

*Jesus went on with his disciples to the villages of Caesarea Philippi; and on the way he asked his disciples, "Who do people say that I am?" And they answered him, "John the Baptist; and others, Elijah; and still others, one of the prophets." He asked them, "But who do you say that I am?" Peter answered him, "You are the Messiah." And he sternly ordered them not to tell anyone about him.*

*Then he began to teach them that the Son of Man must undergo great suffering, and be rejected by the elders, the chief priests, and the scribes, and be killed, and after three days rise again. He said all this quite openly. And Peter took him aside and began to rebuke him. But turning and looking at his disciples, he rebuked Peter and said, "Get behind me, Satan! For you are setting your mind not on divine things, but on human things."*

*And he called the crowd with his disciples, and said to them, "If any want to become my followers,*

*let them deny themselves and take up their cross
and follow me. For those who want to save their life
will lose it, and those who lose their life for my
sake, and for the sake of the gospel, will save it. For
what will it profit them to gain the whole world and
forfeit their life? Indeed, what can they give in
return for their life?"* (Mark 8:27-37)

One of the greatest temptations of any congregation is to compromise with the world's expectations and become some congregation other than the
congregation God is calling it to become. To be sure, it is
a temptation that sooner or later comes to every
congregation. In fact, not even Jesus and his disciples
were exempt from this temptation. Take, for example,
the situation recorded in the above passage of Scripture.
As Jesus and his disciples were on their way to the
villages of Caesarea Philippi, Jesus asked them a very
important question regarding his identity: "Who do
people say that I am?" Jesus, quite obviously, was so
secure in who he was, and what he was about, that he
was not afraid to lift up his life's work for some critical
feedback and evaluation from others.

It is sometimes threatening and painful for us to be the
object of critical reflection and evaluation from others. I
remember when I was a kid growing up in Waco, Texas,
the neighborhood kids would gather on the street corner
at the end of the evening. When it was time for us to go
to our individual homes, none of us wanted to be the first
to leave for fear that those who remained would talk
about us. The only way we found it convenient to leave

one another was for all of us to agree to leave at the same time.

So I am impressed with Jesus. He knew who he was. He knew whose he was. He knew what he was about. He was not afraid to seek some feedback that would give him some idea of how he was being perceived by others.

Likewise, I am impressed with the disciples, because they knew what others were saying about their leader. They evidently had their ears to the ground. They had not only had an encounter with Jesus, they had also had an encounter with the world. It is a reminder to us that among the vital signs in a congregation is not only that it have its ears attuned to the Word, but also that it have its ears attuned to the world. It is a tragedy that the closer some congregations think they are to Jesus, the further they are removed from the world.

So too am I impressed with the disciples. They were with Jesus, but they were also with the people on the streets. And they gave Jesus some feedback in response to his question. They said: "Some say that you are John the Baptist. Some say that you are Elijah. Others say that you are one of the other prophets." Then Jesus asked them: "But who do you say that I am?" And Peter said: "Thou art the Christ." Now, Peter gave the right answer, but he did not understand it. He reminds me of my arithmetic class in elementary school. Often our teacher would give us homework, but I never worried about getting the right answers to the problems. During those days, the answers to all the problems could be found in a section in the back of the book. So all I had to do was to turn to that section for any answer I needed. However, even though I had the correct answers, I could not always explain how I arrived at them. And even though I had the right answers, I lived in fear that the teacher would call on me to explain my answer.

Peter could not explain the answer he gave. Peter's expectation of the Messiah was different than the expectation of the Messiah that God was calling Jesus to become. Peter's expectation of messiahship was shaped by the world's expectations. He had compromised his expectation of the Messiah with the popular expectations of the world. He expected a Messiah who would overthrow the world with military might and power, whereas God had called Jesus to become the Prince of Peace who would transform the world not by violence, but by sacrificial love. Peter did not understand that the answer he gave had cross-bearing consequences. Instead, Peter desired to avoid the cross.

But we are told in Mark 8:30 that Jesus began to teach the disciples that the Son of Man must suffer many things and be rejected by the elders and chief priests and the scribes and be killed and after three days rise again. After hearing this, Peter took Jesus aside and began to rebuke him. In other words, Peter was trying to get Jesus to avoid the cross of sacrificial service and become some messiah other than the Messiah God was calling him to become.

That temptation is still real for the Body of Christ today. John Donders tells about a church in Holland in which the members had a habit of bowing and kneeling before a whitewashed wall in front of the sanctuary before they sat down for worship. None of them knew why they continued this ritual throughout the years. One day the trustees decided to have the whitewashed wall repainted, but before painting the wall, they decided to scrape off the old paint. They were surprised to discover beneath the old paint a centuries-old painting of Jesus on the cross. Somebody had covered up the cross, and it was subsequently lost from memory. The people had forgotten their purpose for bowing and kneeling before they worshiped. Thus they were tempted to become some congregation other than the congregation God was calling them to be. They had kept the ritual, even though it had long since lost its meaning. For the congregation that covers up the cross cannot be a vital and faithful congregation.

It is the same temptation that is faced by the congregation I am now pastoring. When we moved to our present location, we were simply named St. Luke United Methodist Church. We immediately began a process to help us define our identity in our new location. We were preceded in that location by a congregation that left the community when its racial makeup began to change. Thus many people in the vicinity felt forsaken by the church of Jesus Christ. By the same token, they were also suspicious of us.

The question facing us was whether we would live up to our name and become a cross-bearing congregation, or whether we would cover up the cross and forget our reason for bowing and kneeling in worship. Indeed, it would have been arrogant for us to assume that we would be a cross-bearing congregation simply because our racial identity was similar to the majority of the people in our new community. In other words, we were tempted to write off those persons who represented the new minority: Hispanics and elderly whites. To be sure, we could have taken the community for granted and assumed that there would have been no expectations for us to be a cross-bearing community. Furthermore, we were a very small congregation at the time, and we were tempted to adopt a survival and maintenance mode of existence. However, by the grace of God, we gained the courage to call a meeting of our membership in which we dared to raise questions about our identity. The dominant question we raised was: "As the Body of Christ, what kind of congregation is God calling us to become in this particular place?" As we struggled to reach some consensus, one of the words that most frequently informed our conversation was the word *community*. We said that as the people of Jesus Christ, we did not want to hide from the community behind the four walls of the church. We said that we wanted to be a people of God who were engaged in a "come" and "go" affair. We wanted to come to Jesus for worship and nurture, but we also wanted to go for Jesus into the community for witness and service.

In fact, the word *community* became such a vital part of our self-understanding that we literally changed our name to incorporate the word *community*. Thus we became known as St. Luke "Community" United Methodist Church. This word has truly informed our self-understanding; when we are tempted to become a congregation other than the congregation God calls us to be, we always find it helpful to remember who we are.

Indeed, this is what we learned from Jesus in the above passage of Scripture. When Peter tried to get Jesus to be a messiah other than the Messiah God was calling Christ to be, Jesus resisted by saying to Peter:

"Get behind me, Satan." I believe that Jesus was able to resist this great temptation because he remembered who he was. To be sure, his identity was established on the occasion of his baptism by John in the River Jordan. According to Mark 1:10-11, "And just as he was coming up out of the water, he saw the heavens torn apart and the Spirit descending like a dove on him. And a voice came from heaven, 'You are my Son, the Beloved; with you I am well pleased.' " In other words, his identity was clearly defined by God. He knew who he was and his mission was derived out of his identity. When we know who we are, then we know what to do.

Once our congregation defined its identity, we had no problem discovering our mission. In fact, our focus on *community* led us naturally into the following mission statement:

> In the name of Jesus Christ, who is made known to us through the Holy Scriptures, and by the inspiration of the Holy Spirit, we are called to establish, maintain, and nurture a personal relationship with God. We are also called to be a community of God's caring people, within the church and world community, by serving as faithful stewards of our time, talents and money; by combating injustice wherever it may exist; by implementing outreach ministries to meet the needs of the total community; and by our evangelistic witness to the Saviorhood of Jesus Christ, in all that we say and do.

This statement, in turn, led us to more than seventy outreach ministries to our community, including a nutrition program for senior citizens, emergency aid program, a jail ministry, a tutoring program, a single parents group, a drug counseling program, an economic development ministry, and an adopt-a-school program.

Our identity as a cross-bearing people also extended into our personal lives. I remember when I was a kid growing up, when I got old enough to go out in the evenings, my mother never told me what *not* to do. She never said, "Son, don't you smoke dope, don't abuse the girls." She never told me not to disrespect my elders. She never gave me a list of dos and don'ts like that. Instead, as I left home, she would always say, "Son, remember who you are." And as long as I remembered who I was, I never got in trouble. But when I forgot who I was, trouble and I always managed to get together.

Harry Emerson Fosdick, in his autobiography *For the Living of These Days*, tells of the time in his life when he was on the verge of a mental breakdown. He said that, at one point, he was so depressed that he took his father's razor and was about to cut his throat. The only thing that kept him from following through was the voice of his father calling his name: "Harry, Harry, Harry." Fosdick went on to say that when you are in trouble, when you are confused, and when you can't find your way, if somebody close by who loves you will keep on calling you by your right name, you can make it.

Why do we gather for worship? Why do we gather as the church? We gather as the people of God to hear our true names being called. When we are baptized, the heavens break open again and we hear God saying to us, "Thou art my beloved son, thou art my beloved daughter," because God knows our true names.

I think of my forefathers and foremothers in the time of slavery. They were called everything except children of God. But they did not derive their identity from the names that their slave masters called them. Instead, they stole away and they sang a song: "Hush, hush, somebody's calling my name. Hush, hush, somebody's calling my name." And then they sang another verse: "It sounds like Jesus, somebody's calling my name. It sounds like Jesus, somebody's calling my name."

Indeed, later on in more formal times of worship they also especially heard their true names called in the celebration of Holy Communion. The celebration of the Holy Communion is still important in the African American church of any denomination. The very opposite seems to be true in some churches. But in the black community it is the Sunday of largest attendance. How many times have I heard so many of my members say to me: "Pastor, I've got to be there to get my sacrament on the first Sunday." Perhaps part of it has to do with it being, in fact, what it is: a celebration. It is not a solemn funeral for a dead Jesus, but rather a celebration of the risen Lord's victory over the cross, sin, and death. But we first go by the cross before we arrive at the empty tomb. The understanding here is that even though crosses appear and must be borne, there is victory possible. Even though it is Friday now, Sunday does come. The service becomes a mirror not only of life and our day to day experiences, but also a witness and the experience of faith in the One who invites us to his table. Our members leave empowered, renewed, and challenged to depart to serve and to witness, because they have encountered Jesus in the sacrament. Before they leave, we often sing with gusto and enthusiasm and tremendous meaning, "It is well with my soul, / It is well with my soul."

Vital and faithful congregations regularly revisit the places of spiritual renewal and blessedness to encounter Jesus. He can be known in the breaking of bread. He can be encountered in the sacraments if we are open to his presence. The spiritual sets the right mood and tone: "Let us break bread together on our knees." But that spiritual climaxes with the words: "Let us praise God together on our knees!" An encounter with Jesus changes our identity and clarifies our mission.

Several years ago a white pastor in Oklahoma invited me to preach in a revival at a church he was pastoring. It was located in a small farming community. When I arrived, I discovered that he had made arrangements for me to stay in a motel owned and managed by a family from India. Across the street was a locally owned motel. On its marquee were the words: "American owned."

After I preached the first night, few persons shook my hand. While driving me back to the motel for the evening, my host pastor informed me that I was the first African American pastor to preach to his congregation. He also informed me that I was the first guest of the church to be housed in the motel owned by the family from India.

On the next evening I noticed that several African Americans were in the congregation. I was more warmly greeted by the members of the congregation. When my host drove me back to the motel that evening, he told me that that was the first time local African Americans had been invited to participate in their revival. He also told me that he was pleased to observe the warmer reception I received, since some of his leaders had opposed the invitation extended to me.

On each day during the revival, my host pastor took me to a different restaurant for lunch. On the last day, he took me as his guest to a luncheon meeting of the local Kiwanis Club. That evening I discovered that this was the first time an African American had eaten at each of these places.

As I was preparing to leave on the morning after the last evening my host pastor came to see me off. I asked him, "Why did you do this? You did not have to do it!" He replied, "I did it because I believe in the gospel, and I know who I am and whose I am." Then he said, "I want that for my congregation and my community." Then he asked me a question, "Why did you come?" I said to him, "I did not know any better, but now I'm better off for it. For I have heard my true name called!"

By the grace of God, pastors and congregations who know who they are and whose they are in the light of their encounters with Jesus will be faithful congregations who will do the right thing! Let the church say, Amen!

# Encountering Jesus in Seeking Justice

A common tragedy in the life of the church is that many of our members get drunk with the gospel on Sunday. Unfortunately too many of them do not have a spiritual hangover on Monday that makes much difference in the world. No matter how eloquent our preaching, no matter how prolific our programs, our task is unfinished until we make a positive difference on behalf of God's concern for justice in the world.

Several years ago at an annual meeting of the Academy of Homiletics, Art Van Seters highlighted this concern in a paper entitled "Social Hermeneutics Toward a Revolution in Preaching." He said that sexism, racism, classism, and the exploitation of nature are interrelated and contribute to the dehumanization of our time. Governments, laws, business practices, the media, and even Christian churches have rationalized and legitimized oppression, thereby creating a social milieu in which it is difficult to respond to "the gospel in all its liberating power."

"Will preaching, any kind of preaching, in our North American churches, make any difference?" Van Seters asks. He goes on to say that he is bothered that we have accommodated ourselves too easily to a preaching tradition that appeals primarily to thought and emotion, and leaves action up to each individual listener, thereby playing it safe as far as confronting the agonizing issues that daily dehumanize people. This is a way of maintaining the status quo, which is obviously in the self-interest of comfortable churches and their preachers, but hardly consistent with the Jesus who identified with the poor, with women, and with the outcasts of society against the religious establishment of his day, and ended up on a cross.[1]

To be sure, the church's encounter with Jesus on behalf of justice for the poor and oppressed is made sufficiently clear in the parable of the judgment in Matthew 25:31-46. According to the parable, judgment day is a day of separation when the faithful congregations will be distinguished from the unfaithful congregations.

Indeed, a careful reading of the parable reveals some key elements of surprise. The first surprise is the basis upon which Jesus will judge the people gathered before him. As some no doubt expected, he will not judge them on the basis of their theological creeds and doctrines. Nor, as some no doubt expected, will he separate them on the basis of their race, caucus, political affiliation, income, social status, sexual preference, or moral standards. Nor, as some perhaps expected, will Jesus separate them on the basis of how often they prayed, attended worship, tithed, attended church school, or studied the Bible. He did not even separate them on the basis of whether they were baptized by sprinkling, pouring, or immersion; or whether or not they had been anointed with oil; or whether or not they shouted praises and said "Amen!" Nor did Jesus separate them on the basis of whether or not they were church officers and leaders. Instead, the surprising and only basis was whether or not they ministered to the poor and oppressed.

> Then the king will say to those at his right hand, "Come, you that are blessed by my Father, inherit the kingdom prepared for you from the foundation of the world; for I was hungry and you gave me food, I was thirsty and you gave me something to drink, I was a stranger and you welcomed me, I was naked and you gave me clothing, I was sick and you took care of me, I was in prison and you visited me." Then the righteous will answer him, "Lord, when was it that we saw you hungry and gave you food, or thirsty and gave you something to drink? And when was it that we saw you a stranger and welcomed you, or naked and gave you clothing? And when was it that we saw you sick or in prison and visited you?" And the king will answer them, "Truly I tell you, just as you did it to one of the least of these who are members of my family, you did it to me." (Matthew 25:34-40)

Now if service on behalf of these poor and oppressed is the only basis used to distinguish between the faithful and the unfaithful, does this mean that morality, worship, prayer, Bible study, church school, baptism, speaking in tongues, and gifts of the Spirit are unimportant? No, they are very important. But if they do not inspire us to serve the cause of justice on behalf of the poor and the oppressed, they become ends in themselves and make us good for nothing!

It's the same theme as that sounded by Paul in I Corinthians 13:1-3: "If I speak in the tongues of mortals and of angels, but do not have love, I am a noisy gong or a clanging cymbal. And if I have prophetic powers, and understand all mysteries and all knowledge, and if I have all faith, so as to remove mountains, but do not have love, I am nothing. If I give away all my possessions, and if I hand over my body so that I may boast, but do not have love, I gain nothing."

The theme is repeated in the letter of James: "What good is it brothers and sisters, if you say you have faith but do not have works? Can faith save you? If a brother or sister is naked and lacks daily food, and one of you says to them, 'Go in peace; keep warm and eat your fill,' and yet you do not supply their bodily needs, what is the good of that? So faith by itself, if it has no works, is dead" (James 2:14-17). More important, when faith tries to live without works, it is not just faith that dies, it is the poor and oppressed who also die.

This is precisely why *individual* acts of charity cannot be substitutes for *collective* acts of justice. To be sure, individual acts of charity are necessary responses to injustice; but they do not challenge the reasons for injustice.

In this context, it is significant to note that Jesus does not address the parable of the last judgment to isolated individuals. Instead, the parable is addressed to the nations! According to Matthew 25:32: "All the nations will be gathered before him, and he will separate people one from another as a shepherd separates the sheep from the goats." In other words, Jesus encounters us and places us on trial not only in terms of our individual and separate accountability, but also in terms of our corporate and congregational accountability. He is calling us to challenge social structures of injustice, as well as provide handouts for individual victims of injustice. In fact, tribes, cities, races, and nations are called to accountability throughout Scripture on behalf of the poor and the oppressed.

Ron Sider tells of a group of devout Christians who lived in a small village at the foot of a mountain. A winding, slippery road with hairpin curves and deep precipices without guard rails wound its way up on one side of the mountain and down the other. Consequently, there were frequent accidents that proved to be fatal. Deeply saddened by the injured people who were pulled from the wrecked cars, the Christians in the village's three churches decided to act. They pooled their resources and purchased an ambulance so that they could rush the injured to the hospital in the next town. Week after week church volunteers gave faithfully, even sacrificially, of their time to operate the ambulance twenty-four hours a day. They saved many lives, although some victims remained crippled for life.

Then one day a young visitor came to town. Puzzled, he asked why they did not close the road over the mountain and build a tunnel instead. Startled at first, the ambulance volunteers quickly pointed out that this approach, although technically possible, was not realistic or advisable. After all, the narrow mountain road had been there for a long time. Besides, they noted, the mayor would bitterly oppose the idea since he owned a large restaurant and service station halfway up the mountain.

The visitor was shocked that the mayor's economic interests mattered more to these Christians than the many human casualties. Somewhat hesitantly, he suggested that perhaps the churches ought to speak to the mayor. After all, he was an elder in the oldest church in town. Perhaps they should elect a different mayor if he proved to be stubborn and unconcerned. Now the Christians were shocked. With rising indignation and righteous conviction they informed the young "radical" that the church dare not become involved in politics. They said the church is called to preach the gospel and give a cup of cold water. Its mission, they said is not to dabble in worldly things like social and political structures.

Perplexed and bitter, the stranger left. As he wandered out of the village, one question churned around and around in his mind. Is it really more spiritual, he wondered, to operate the ambulance that picks up the bloody victims of destructive social structures than to try to change the structures themselves?[2]

The questions of ethics and injustice and some of the "nasty realities of life" require the church to clearly distinguish between charity and justice. For the practice of charity and the pursuit of justice are not the same. Charity is essentially a temporary provision. It may provide temporary relief; however, it does not deal with the root causes of the problem.

The parable of the good Samaritan is a classic example of a charitable response. The parable does not speak about any attempt on the part of the good Samaritan to do anything about the root causes of highway robbery. He did nothing to provide better road conditions and security measures that would help prevent robberies. He did nothing to provide reform efforts for the robbers or to provide better job conditions for would-be robbers. Nor did he do anything to eliminate the economic disparity between the haves and the have-nots. He took the wounded man to an inn to provide for his temporary needs. And that was important at that given moment— certainly to the man who was wounded.

However, justice goes beyond the inn. It demands a different set of responses. It seeks to remove and remedy root causes. To be sure, sometimes radical change is demanded. For example, if one is on a train and is moving in the wrong direction, it does no good to run down the aisle in the opposite direction. Instead, one has to get off the train or work to get it turned around so it can move in the right direction.

If Moses had been content with nothing but charitable relief measures for his fellow Hebrews who were enslaved in Egypt, they would not have experienced liberation. They would have still been in Egypt enslaved under Pharaoh with bandaged wounds and balm on their whip-lashed sores. But Moses moved beyond charity to justice. He challenged the institutional and structural injustices of Pharaoh's system, even disobeying unjust Egyptian laws, and ultimately led his people to a new freedom and a new identity.

This is not to suggest that congregations should abandon acts of charity and works of mercy, but rather that these acts should be done in such a way that the charitable act does not negate the demands for justice. As a matter of fact, charity and justice need each other. Indeed, one complements the other for the sake of the liberation and salvation of the poor and the oppressed in the name of Jesus. When people are bleeding, they do not want to be told that their bleeding is only a symptom that they have been stabbed. They want us to give them a tourniquet and a bandage. They do not want us to tell them that we cannot do anything until we can find a cure for the root cause of violence. They want us to provide immediate first-aid while we attempt to address the systemic problem.

William Hulme refers to charity and justice as true ways of congregations caring. While a seminary student, he taught a Sunday school class for a group of boys in a slum area. He had little support from their families and had to contend with the fact that no one would wake up on time for class. So he took on the responsibility himself. Each Sunday morning, he left home an hour or so early to go from house to house, often entering the room where one of the boys was still asleep.

Hulme says that on one occasion one of the boys said something that changed his congregational approach to ministry. He thanked Hulme for his interest, but the boy advised Hulme to forget about him. The boy said to him, "It's no use, Bill, because you can't live in this neighborhood and also be a Christian." Hulme said that he and his congregation learned that it was not enough for them to teach the boys about Christ; they also had to engage in acts of justice on behalf of that blighted neighborhood. "Poverty," he later wrote, "was more than a lack of material goods. It was an empowering social force that distorted and stunted the lives of those who were trapped under its weight."[3]

Leonardo Boff, in his book *Way of the Cross—Way of Justice,* speaks of seeking God's reign:

> Pious human beings will always ask: Where do we find God? Religions mark out the main places and the privileged situations in which we encounter God, e.g., prayer, the interior life, a lifestyle of simplicity and asceticism, and unselfish service to our fellow human beings. . . .
>
>   Christians know that they encounter God in the Church, in its sacraments, in the sacred words of Scripture and in the fraternal loving encounter with their neighbors.[4]

The question is legitimate; where do we find God? The answers given above are relevant. But we learn from Jesus that the truly basic question is a different one: Where does God want to be encountered by human beings?[5]

The words keep echoing in my head from the New Testament and the image won't go away: "I was hungry and you gave me food, I was thirsty and you gave me something to drink, I was a stranger and you welcomed me, I was naked and you gave me clothing, I was sick and you took care of me; I was in prison and you visited me" (Matthew 25:35-36).

# Getting It All Together (In the Name of Jesus)

*They came to the other side of the sea, to the country of the Gerasenes. And when he had stepped out of the boat, immediately a man out of the tombs with an unclean spirit met him. He lived among the tombs; and no one could restrain him any more, even with a chain; for he had often been restrained with shackles and chains, but the chains he wrenched apart, and the shackles he broke in pieces; and no one had the strength to subdue him. Night and day among the tombs and on the mountains he was always howling and bruising himself with stones. When he saw Jesus from a distance, he ran and bowed down before him; and he shouted at the top of his voice, "What have you to do with me, Jesus, Son of the Most High God?"* (Mark 5:1-7)

In this passage we are introduced to a man who quite obviously did not "have it all together"! To be sure, in the worst sort of way, his life was disorganized, diseased, and disconnected. He was separated from his best self. He was separated from his family. He was separated from his community. He was separated from his church. Indeed, he was separated from Jesus! And yet this is not to say that his life was without significant worth and intrinsic value. Chances are he had been blessed by God with outstanding talents and potential. Chances are that he had been blessed by God with a gifted mind. He may have even been blessed by God with many other desirable attributes and qualities. But no matter what gifts, talents, and resources he may have had, they were not doing him or anybody else any good, simply because he was unable to get them all together and marshal them toward some clear, singular, and positive direction for the sake of the kingdom of God.

I believe this man's condition is quite symbolic of many individuals and institutions in our world today. He reminds me of a former college classmate of mine. He was gifted and talented. He had a brilliant mind. He was wealthy. He excelled in extracurricular activities. He was handsome and good looking. All the girls loved him! He had so much going for him. And yet, in spite of all his blessings, he wandered from career to career, from goal to goal, from school to school, never able to get all of his gifts and resources together and marshal them toward some clear, singular, and positive direction. By his own admission, he confessed that he could not find the organizing principles around which he could focus his life so that he could move in some positive direction.

I believe the condition of this man in Mark's Gospel is also symbolic of our world condition. When I view our world, on the one hand I see a world that has been richly blessed by God with a technicolor panorama of precious people, resources, and an abundant display of natural resources. In fact, after God created and reviewed the earth, God said it was good (Genesis 1:21). But on the other hand, our world's condition is shaped by militarism, racism, sexism, brokenness, homelessness, parochialism, hunger, drug and substance abuse, and poverty. Why is this true? Surely not because God has failed to provide abundant resources for our well-being and our welfare. The God-given resources are available. The problem is our failure to get all our God-given resources together so that we can marshal them toward some clear, singular, and positive direction for good.

In his last book, *Where Do We Go from Here? Chaos or Community?* the late Dr. Martin Luther King, Jr., tells of a famous novelist who died several years ago, leaving a suggested list of plots for future stories. Dr. King said that especially notable among them was this one: "A widely separated family inherits a great world house in which they have to live together." Commenting on this suggested plot, Dr. King said: "This is the great problem of humankind. We have inherited a great world house in which we have to live together: black, white, brown, yellow, and red; easterner and westerner; Gentile and Jew, Protestant and Catholic, Muslim and Hindu; a family unduly separated in idea, culture and interest, who because we can never again live apart, must somehow learn to live with each other in peace."[1] Thus, the challenge for our world is: How, by God's grace can we get all God's healing and reconciling gifts together so that we may move them toward some clear, singular, and positive direction for the sake of the kingdom of God?

I believe that the condition of the man with the
unclean spirit in Mark's Gospel is symbolic of my own
United Methodist denomination. On the one hand,
when I look at the denomination, I see a church that has
been blessed by God with a marvelous gift of human
resources. To be sure, our denomination is one of the
most racially and ethnically pluralistic predominantly
white denominations in America today. If there were no
whites or Native Americans in the United Methodist
Church, we would be one of the largest Asian American
denominations in America today. If there were no
whites, Native Americans, or no Asian Americans in the
United Methodist Church, we would be the third
largest Spanish-speaking denomination in America
today. If there were no whites, Native Americans, Asian
Americans, or Hispanic Americans in the United
Methodist Church, we would be the seventh largest
African American denomination in America today.

What a precious gift of people resources! But it too is a
gift with a challenge—namely, how can we get our
God-given human resources together so that we may
move them toward a clear, singular, and positive
direction for the sake of the kingdom of God?

The challenge we hold in common with the man in
Mark's Gospel reminds me of the story of the man who
went shopping and bought himself a new pair of pants.
When he got home he discovered that the pants were
two inches too long. He wanted to wear them to work
the next morning. So he asked his wife if she would cut
off two inches and hem them. But she said she was too
tired, excused herself, and went to bed. The man then
turned to his mother-in-law for help. She too informed

him that she had had a hard day and excused herself and went to bed. The man had no choice left to him but to fix the pants himself. He took the pants, cut off two inches, hemmed the pants, and placed them across a chair and went to bed himself. Around twelve o'clock his wife woke up with a change of heart. So she got up, cut off two more inches of pants, hemmed them, placed them back across the chair, and went back to bed. An hour or so later, his mother-in-law woke up with a change of heart. She got up, found the pants, cut off two more inches, hemmed the pants, placed them across the chair where she had found them, and went back to bed. Well, you can imagine how the man felt the next morning when he got up and found that instead of pants to wear to his office, he had *walking shorts!*

Likewise, this is what happens when we cannot get it all together in the church and the world. We end up shortchanging those whom God has called us to serve, simply because we have difficulty finding the organizing principle around which we can gather our God-given resources and marshal them toward some clear, singular, and positive direction for the sake of the Kingdom.

When we cannot get it all together, our greatest need is a fresh encounter with Jesus. This is the testimony of Mark's Gospel in the story of the Gerasene demoniac. In the midst of the Gerasene demoniac, Jesus took the initiative to make his presence known. He knows our need. He knows that we cannot be as productive as God wants us to be without him. In the face of our brokenness, he challenges us to get it all together, so that as the people of God we may move in a clear, singular, and positive direction for the sake of the Kingdom.

In his encounter with the Gerasene demoniac, Jesus asks him, "What is your name?" The demoniac replies, "My name is Legion." *Legion* is the Latin word for an army battalion of 6,000 soldiers. In other words, I take this to mean that the man was saying: "I don't know which is the real me! I am so many different people. I am this one today or now. Another day or another time I am somebody else. My deeds don't match my creeds. My lip service does not match my love service. My principles do not match my practices. I can talk that talk! But I can't walk that walk!"

However, the testimony of Mark's Gospel is that Jesus has authority and power over the demoniac powers that seek to keep us from getting our life together. Indeed, this story in the fifth chapter of Mark functions as a resurrection passage. For the demoniac has a life-changing encounter with Jesus, who becomes the organizing center that enables him to overcome the demoniac forces and move his life in a clear, singular, and positive direction. In fact, when the people in his community came to see what had happened, they came to Jesus and found the demoniac sitting there, clothed and in his right mind (v. 15).

I shall never forget the time my father took me to my first symphony concert. I was nine years old. The concert was held on the campus of Baylor University in Waco, Texas. This was during the time of rigid segregation in Texas and in the nation. So my father and I had to sit in the balcony, where people who were not white were forced to sit. As I took my seat and looked down upon the stage, I immediately became perplexed and confused by the noise of the instruments. I noticed that each of the musicians was playing different and uncoordinated sounds on different instruments. Each trumpet player was playing his own tune. It was likewise, with the violinists and the other instrumentalists.

I became so confused that I eventually turned to my father and asked him, "Dad, what is going on?" My father patted me on my head and said, "Be quiet, Son, this is just the warm-up period!" I obeyed my father and remained quiet, but I still did not understand what was going on.

After a while a little man came out on the stage, stood before the orchestra, and held up a baton. All of a sudden there was complete silence throughout the whole great hall.

Then in the midst of the silence the conductor began to wave his baton. And oh, the transformation that took place. Distractions became attractions. Noise became praise! Disunity became unity. Jangling discords became beautiful choirs of harmony! Separate solos became shared symphony! Conflicting sounds became cooperating sounds.

What made the difference? The difference was caused by the fact that instead of each orchestra member playing his or her own separate tune, each member now took his or her cue from one common master, no matter what instrument he or she played. The common director had become the organizing center that enabled the symphony to "get it all together."

An on-going encounter with Jesus is the centerpiece of faithful and vital congregations. When we turn our eyes upon Jesus, and focus on his face, the other many things become strangely dim and hard to see because of the brightness and the glory and the clarity of his grace and direction. Our faulty focus becomes clear. When all eyes are upon him and we take our cue from him, the people of God are enabled to celebrate their God-given resources and move them in a clear, singular, and positive direction for the sake of the Kingdom.

> And being found in human form,
>     he humbled himself
>     and became obedient to the point of death—
>     even death on a cross.
> Therefore God also highly exalted him
>     and gave him the name
>     that is above every name,
> so that at the name of Jesus
>     every knee should bend,
>     in heaven and on earth and under the earth,
> and every tongue should confess
>     that Jesus Christ is Lord,
>     to the glory of God the Father.
>                           (Philippians 2:7*b*-11)

> All hail the power of Jesus' name!
> Let angels prostrate fall;
> Bring forth the royal diadem,
> And crown him Lord of all.

# 1. Encounters That Count

1. Albert Schweitzer, *Quest of the Historical Jesus* (New York: Macmillan, 1964), p. 403]

# 2. Encountering Jesus in the Bible

1. William H. Willimon, *Shaped by the Bible* (Nashville: Abingdon Press, 1990), p. 13.
2. Quoted in Albert J. Raboteau, *Slave Religion* (Oxford: Oxford University Press, 1978), p. 240.
3. Ibid.
4. Martin E. Marty, "How My Mind Has Changed," *The Christian Century*, July 10-17, 1991, p. 703.

# 3. Encountering Jesus in Worship

1. Clarence Joseph Rivers, *The Spirit in Worship* (Cincinnati: Stimuli, Inc., 1978), p. 16.
2. Ibid.
3. Frank C. Senn, *Christian Worship and Its Cultural Setting* (Philadelphia: Fortress Press, 1983), p. 4.
4. Franz Hildebrandt and Oliver A. Beckerlegge, eds. *A Collection of Hymns for the Use of the People Called Methodists* in *The Works of John Wesley* (Nashville: Abingdon Press, 1988), p. 81.

5. See William B. McClain, *Come Sunday: The Liturgy of Zion* (Nashville: Abingdon Press, 1990), especially chapter 5, "Black Preaching and Its Message: Is There Any Word from the Lord?" pp. 59-71. See also William D. Watley, *Preaching on Special Occasions* (Valley Forge: Judson Press, 1989), and Henry Mitchell *The Art of Black Preaching* (Nashville: Abingdon Press, 1990).

## 4. Encountering Jesus in Preaching

1. P. T. Forsyth, *Positive Preaching and the Modern Mind* (New York: Hodder and Stoughton, 1907), p. 53.
2. Thomas H. Troeger, "What Shall I Preach On Sunday?" in *The Christian Century*, March, 1980, p. 5.
3. Justo L. Gonzalez and Catherine Gonzalez, *Liberation Preaching* (Nashville: Abingdon Press, 1980), p. 48.
4. Ibid., p. 50.
5. Ibid.
6. Dietrich Ritschl, *A Theology of Proclamation* (Richmond: John Knox Press, 1960), p. 33.
7. Henry Mitchell, *The Recovery of Preaching* (San Francisco: Harper & Row, 1977), pp. 115-16.
8. Reuel Howe, *Partners in Preaching* (New York: Seabury Press, 1967), pp. 26-29.
9. Troeger, "What Shall I Preach on Sunday?" in *The Christian Century*, March, 1980, p. 5.
10. Karl Barth, *How I Changed My Mind*, introduction and epilogue by John D. Godsey (Richmond: John Knox Press, 1966), p. 12.
11. Mitchell, *The Recovery of Preaching*, p. 5.
12. Troeger, "What Shall I Preach on Sunday?" pp. 7-8.
13. Quoted in George E. Sweazy, *Preaching the Good News* (Englewood Cliffs, N.J.: Prentice-Hall, 1976), p. 312.

## 6. Encountering Jesus in Seeking Justice

1. Arthur Van Seters, "Social Hermeneutics Toward a Revolution in Preaching," paper delivered at the 1981 Annual Meeting of the Academy of Homiletics.
2. Ronald J. Sider, *Rich Christians in An Age of Hunger* (Waco, Tex.: Word Books, 1990), pp. 203-4.
3. William E. Hulme, *Two Ways of Caring* (Minneapolis: Augsburg Press, 1973), pp. 8-9.

4. Leonardo Boff, *Way of the Cross: Way of Justice,* trans. John Drury (Maryknoll, N.Y.: Orbis Books, 1986), p. 46.
5. Ibid.

## 7. Getting It All Together

1. Martin Luther King, Jr., *Where Do We Go From Here: Chaos or Community?* (New York: Harper & Row, 1967).

# Suggestions for Leading a Study of *Encountering Jesus*

*Encountering Jesus* offers many practical ideas for helping individuals and congregations become more effective ministers. As a discussion leader, you have the opportunity to help the members of your group grow in faith and in service to others. Here are some suggestions to keep in mind as you begin this adventure:

1. You should read the entire book before your first group meeting so you have an overview of your journey and can be a better guide for the members of your group. You may want to use a highlighter to designate important points.

2. Hand out the book to participants before the first session and ask them to have read the first chapter before your initial meeting. You may want to limit the size of your group to less than ten members so everyone gets a chance to participate.

3. Begin each session by reviewing the main points using the chapter summary. You may ask group members for what they saw as highlights. Use your leader's guide to suggest other main points.

4. Select the discussion questions and activities in advance. Use the ones you think will work best. You may want to ask the questions in a different order from how they are listed in the leader's guide. Allow a set amount of time for questions and a set amount of time for one or two activities. Create your own questions or activity if you desire.

5. Before moving from questions to activities, ask members if they have any questions that have not been answered.

6. Following conclusion of the activity, close with a short prayer. If your group desires, pause for individual prayer petitions.

7. Start your meetings on time and end them on schedule.

8. If you ask a question and no one volunteers an answer, begin the discussion by suggesting an answer yourself. Then ask for comments and other answers.

9. Encourage total participation by asking questions of specific

members. Your role is to give everyone who wants to a chance to talk. Remember you can always ask the question "Why?" to continue a discussion.

10. Be thankful and supportive. Thank members for their ideas and participation.

## CHAPTER 1

# Encounters That Count

## Chapter Summary

- ▶ To encounter Jesus is to take the name of Christ.
- ▶ We need to be intentional. We need to have an awareness of why we are doing what we are doing.
- ▶ We can encounter Jesus in familiar places: the Bible, worship, baptism, the Eucharist, in the life of the church, and so on.
- ▶ To encounter Jesus and have a real exchange with God is the real business of the church.
- ▶ This book is written to explore how we encounter Jesus.

## Discussion Questions

1. What new thought or idea did you encounter while reading this first chapter?
2. What are people looking for when they seek to encounter Jesus?
3. Why does Jesus want us to have an encounter with him?
4. What does it mean to have an encounter with Jesus?
5. Where do we hear the name of Jesus outside of church?
6. Name one of your past encounters with Jesus.
7. How can we be more intentional in our encounters?
8. Where do we encounter Jesus today?
9. Where do we *not* encounter Jesus today?
10. What are the risks of daring to speak the name of Jesus?
11. How would you define the word *encounter*?
12. How do people and churches avoid encountering Jesus?

## Practical Applications / Activities

▶ Write a mission statement for your group. What goals do you want to accomplish as you read this book?

▶ List ways that your church presently encourages encounters with Jesus.

▶ How many times does the name of Jesus appear in your church newsletter?

▶ List some encounters from the Bible that Jesus had with people. How were the people changed?

▶ Keep a list this week of how many times you saw or heard the name of Jesus outside of church.

**Prayer:** *Jesus, we thank you for giving us the opportunity to have a real encounter with you and for increasing our awareness of how we can be more effective as individuals and as your church in witnessing to others. Open our eyes and ears so that we may see and hear you this week. Grant us the wisdom to learn how we can become more vital in ministry and take action guided by your Holy Spirit. In the Name of Jesus, Amen.*

# Encountering Jesus in the Bible

## Chapter Summary

▶ We encounter Jesus through the Bible.

▶ Congregations become vital and faithful by studying the Bible.

▶ Reading the Bible starts new dialogues and conversations within the church.

▶ Reading the Bible challenges us to grow as Christians, to ask tough questions and search for answers.

▶ The Bible helps God speak to us. It opens the line of communication.

## Discussion Questions

1. What new idea did you have while reading this chapter?
2. How can the Bible be used to encounter Jesus?
3. How can we increase our encounters with Jesus while reading the Bible?
4. What are reasons people do not read the Bible?
5. List benefits of individual participation in a Bible study.
6. How are congregations changed by serious use and study of the Bible?
7. How has reading the Bible changed your life?
8. Is it easier to read the Bible alone or in a group?
9. Why do you read the Bible?
10. Who influenced you to read the Bible?
11. How has the Bible changed over the years? Why?
12. If you would recommend one book of the BIble to read, which book would it be? Why?

## Practical Applications / Activities

▶ Find verses in the Bible that speak about the blessings of studying God's Word.

▶ Plan a "Bible census" at your church to see if enough people have access to Bibles and to redistribute extra Bibles.

▶ Discuss ways the youth of the church can be encouraged to read the Bible.

▶ Bring up the Bible in conversation at home or work this week and note the reaction.

▶ How can use of the Bible be increased during the worship service?

**Prayer:** *Jesus, we thank you for the gift of the Bible and the blessings that it gives us. Help us to use the Bible to encounter you and learn of your will for our lives and for our church. Slow us down so we take the time to pray and listen to you. Stir us to action in our church and within our community out of love for others and for you. May your Holy Word awaken us to faith's demands and rich promises. In the Name of Jesus, Amen.*

## CHAPTER 3

# Encountering Jesus in Worship

## Chapter Summary

- ▶ The purpose of worship is to gather in Christ's name, to encounter Jesus.
- ▶ Worship is hard work. It demands something from us as it gives something to us.
- ▶ Worship is a response to what God has already done for us in Jesus Christ. It is a response of praise.
- ▶ We come to worship not to seek God, but to be found by God.
- ▶ Worship loses its value when it becomes an end in itself and does not send participants out into the world to engage in Christian service.

## Discussion Questions

1. What did you learn about worship that you had not known before?
2. In what ways do we encounter Jesus in worship?
3. What is a common weakness in most worship services?
4. What do you personally get the most out of in worship?
5. How should a person feel at the conclusion of a worship service?
6. How does a person prepare for worship?
7. What are the causes of failure to encounter Jesus in a worship service?
8. What part should the Bible play in worship?
9. How could one person make a difference at a worship service?
10. What fuels worship?
11. How do we speak to God in worship?
12. How do we listen to God in worship?

## Practical Applications / Activities

- ▶ Develop a list of worship criteria. (See the last paragraph of this chapter for examples.)
- ▶ As a group, discuss ways your congregation could be educated about worship.
- ▶ List three ways worship at your church could be improved.
- ▶ List what your church does well in worship.
- ▶ Brainstorm ways your church could be more welcoming and inclusive in worship.

**Prayer:** *Jesus, we thank you for the privilege of encountering you in worship. Please help us to learn in worship to draw closer to you so we can go out into the world in Christian service. We praise you for your constant love and your many blessings, especially for this opportunity to explore how we can become a more vital and faithful church. Open our eyes to the needs of this church and grant us the wisdom to do your will. In Jesus' Name. Amen.*

CHAPTER 4

# Encountering Jesus in Preaching

## Chapter Summary

▶ Preaching is a cooperative effort between the pulpit and the pew.

▶ Preaching is issuing an invitation to have an encounter with Jesus.

▶ Our task is not to introduce the Word, but to expose the Word that is already there.

▶ The pastor needs to listen to the preaching congregation and to hear their needs.

▶ Ministry belongs to the whole church.

## Discussion Questions

1. What new thought or idea about preaching did you encounter while reading this chapter?
2. What role does listening play for the preacher?
3. What role does listening play for the congregation?
4. What does "preaching congregation" mean to you?
5. Name ways we encounter Jesus through preaching.
6. In what ways do we apply church doctrine to life rather than discover doctrine in life?
7. What are keys to making preaching portable and repeatable?
8. What are traits of constructive feedback and evaluation?
9. How can a congregation uplift a preacher during the sermon?
10. How can a congregation prepare to receive a sermon?
11. How is the Bible to be used in preaching?
12. Name a sermon that had an impact on you. Tell why

## Practical Applications / Activities

▶ Name specific ways church members can become more of a preaching congregation.

- ▶ Brainstorm ways you can educate members about their role in preaching.
- ▶ Discuss ways this group can help the pastor be a more effective preacher.
- ▶ What is this church doing right when it comes to preaching?
- ▶ Write a list of sermon ingredients and traits.

---

**Prayer:** *Jesus, we thank you how your Word touches our lives through preaching. Help us to remember we are all preachers and carry your good news with us at all times. We ask that this church become a stronger preaching congregation so more people will encounter you and learn about your love. Increase in us our knowledge of you and your will for this church. We ask this in your Holy Name. Amen.*

## CHAPTER 5

# Encountering Jesus in the Life of the Church and the Community

## Chapter Summary

▶ One of the greatest temptations for a congregation is to become what the world, not God, wants it to become.

▶ The ears of a congregation need to be tuned to the Word and the world.

▶ Once a church defines its identity, it can discover its mission.

▶ We gather as a church community to hear our own names being called.

▶ Our identity as a cross-bearing people must be extended to our personal lives.

## Discussion Questions

1. What new thought or idea did you encounter in this chapter?
2. Why does the author begin this chapter with Mark 8:27-37?
3. Name ways in which we hear our true names being called.
4. What are the benefits of knowing our true identity?
5. How can churches become tempted by the world?
6. How can we discover what God is calling our congregation to become?
7. Where do we encounter Jesus within our community?
8. Name some "church rituals."
9. What questions are difficult to raise within a church? Why?
10. How is the mission of a church connected to location?
11. How is the church like a mirror?
12. How is our church presently reaching out to the community?

## Practical Applications / Activities

▶ Review your church mission statement as a group and see if it needs updating. If none exists, brainstorm what it could say.

▶ List ten needs of your community, then list some possible new ministries for your church.

▶ As a group project, ask the residents of nearby homes what they think about your church and if your church is a good neighbor.

▶ Define the minority in your congregation. How are they supported?

▶ Discuss how the name of your church was chosen and how you feel about your church name.

*Prayer:* Jesus, we thank you for the many opportunities for ministry within our community and for placing us and our church in this place for the purpose of helping our neighbors encounter you. Help us to remember our identity and our calling so we can accomplish your will for our church. Let our ears be listening to your Word and the needs of our world. Grant us wisdom and courage to act as you show us what needs to be done. In the Name of Jesus, Amen.

## CHAPTER 6

# Encountering Jesus in Seeking Justice

## Chapter Summary

▶ True justice seeks to remedy and remove root causes.

▶ The church needs to inspire members to serve the cause of injustice on behalf of the poor.

▶ Charitable acts should not negate demands for justice.

▶ We need to challenge the reasons of injustice.

▶ Individual acts of charity cannot substitute for collective acts of justice.

## Discussion Questions

1. What new thought or idea did you encounter?
2. Why is charity only a temporary provision?
3. List some causes of injustice.
4. How can a church inspire members and their community to serve the cause of justice?
5. How can injustice be challenged by the church?
6. What does it mean for a church to go beyond charity?
7. What prevents us as Christians and as a church from seeking justice?
8. What are the costs of justice and the costs of injustice?
9. How do church funds (offerings) fight injustice?
10. Who are the unwanted neighbors in our community?
11. What issues of justice affect the elderly?
12. What resources does a church have to fight injustice?

## Practical Applications/ Activities

▶ As a group, find examples of charity and justice in the Bible.

▶ Use a current newspaper to locate news that relates to justice and charity in your area.

▶ Plan a congregational forum on this issue.

- ▶ Identify five local agencies/charities that could use the help of your congregation. Visit one organization.
- ▶ Discuss different ways this issue can be presented to your congregation. How can you educate members?

*Prayer:* Jesus, we thank and praise you for your concern for all people in this world. No one is forgotten by you. Help us to challenge injustice and perform acts of charity in your name. Give us ears to hear and eyes to see those who need to encounter you. Grant our church the strength to take a stand on community issues and see that all those around us are brothers and sisters. We ask this in your Holy Name. Amen.

## CHAPTER 7

# Getting It All Together
# (In the Name of Jesus)

## Chapter Summary

▶ An ongoing encounter with Jesus is the centerpiece of faithful and vital congregations.

▶ Jesus challenges us to move forward with him.

▶ Jesus knows what we need and empowers us in ministry.

▶ Jesus has power over what prevents us from moving ahead in ministry.

▶ When we encounter Jesus, we encounter love in action that we pass on to others.

## Discussion Questions

1. What challenged you in this chapter?
2. What lessons do we learn from the man in Mark's Gospel?
3. What does it cost to encounter Jesus?
4. What does it take to keep the encounter ongoing?
5. How does God unify and lead us through Christ?
6. What prevents us as a church from getting it all together?
7. How can we encounter change at our church?
8. What is the first step toward having an encounter?
9. What would you like our next encounter with Jesus to be?
10. How has your thinking changed as a result of reading this book?
11. What partners can we team with in encountering Jesus?
12. What in this book helped you the most?

## Practical Applications / Activities

▶ List the resources of your church and the resources of individual members.

- ▶ Brainstorm specific ideas for creating a vital and faithful congregation.
- ▶ Write your own personal mission statement. Share it with the group, if you desire.
- ▶ Write a list of what you have learned about encountering Jesus.
- ▶ Write an article for your church newsletter about your study of this book.

---

**Prayer:** Jesus, we are grateful for encountering you and your love while reading this book and through our discussions. Help us to take what we have learned and use it to make a difference in our church and in our community. We want to become vital and faithful ministers. Empower us to become a preaching congregation that opens the hearts, eyes, and ears of people so they may come to know you. We thank you for this time together and ask your blessing as we begin to implement what we have learned. In the Name of Jesus, Amen.